Pondering Solutions
to the King Snake Puzzle

An Adventure in Discrete Mathematics

By **Ellen Starbuck**

ARCHWAY
PUBLISHING

Bloomington, Indiana, USA

Archway Publishing books may be ordered through booksellers or by contacting:

Archway Publishing
1663 Liberty Drive
Bloomington, IN 47403
www.archwaypublishing.com
844-669-3957

Because of the dynamic nature of the Internet, any web addresses or links contained in this book may have changed since publication and may no longer be valid. The views expressed in this work are solely those of the author and do not necessarily reflect the views of the publisher, and the publisher hereby disclaims any responsibility for them.

ISBN: 978-1-6657-6951-8 (sc)
ISBN: 978-1-6657-6950-1 (hc)

Library of Congress Control Number: 2024926480

Print information available on the last page.

Archway Publishing rev. date: 04/21/2025

==

Genre: Academic

==

BISG, Book Industry Study Group

BISAC Subject Headings List
Want to find a code to categorize a book? The BISAC Subject Codes List* (or BISAC Subject Headings) is the US standard topical categorization used by companies throughout the supply chain. The Subject Heading applied to a book can determine where the work is shelved in a brick and mortar store or the genre(s) under which it can be searched for in an internal database.

Some BISAC codes applicable to this workbook:
COM051200 Computers/Languages/Visual Basic
COM051300 Computers/Programming/Algorithms
MAT008000 Mathematics/Discrete Mathematics
GAM007000 Games and Activities/Puzzles

About the Author

One Sunday afternoon in 1947, in a Chinese restaurant in Jacksonville, Florida, Ms. Starbuck was given the little wooden elephant puzzle. She has been attracted to take-apart/put-together puzzles since that time. Her current favorites are the six-piece burr, Stewart Coffin's "Three-piece Block," and the snake puzzles, the 27-cube snake as well as the 64-cube.

Ms. Starbuck's formal studies include Mathematics at Florida State University, B.A. 1958, and Computer Science in the School of Engineering at U.C.L.A., 1968-1970.

In 1959, Ms. Starbuck went to work for the System Development Corporation* in Santa Monica, California, with the job title "Computer Programmer". Her first computer was the AN/FSQ-7,* an "automatic" device in the SAGE* system (Semi-Automatic Ground Environment*). She spent the whole of her professional career developing software systems, primarily for agencies of the Federal Government.

Shortly after Ms. Starbuck went to work in Santa Monica, she wrote to a school buddy whom she had left back home in Florida, "Come work with me. Come help us build this software system. It's like solving puzzles all day."

To contact Ms. Starbuck, send e-mail to CuriousPuzzler@outlook.com.

* Look it up in Wikipedia.

Forewords

Some years ago, my path crossed Ellen's. I soon learned that Ellen has a love of puzzles and riddles. A couple of years ago, she introduced me to the 27-cube Snake puzzle. Even with her list of steps for solving it, I had a difficult time at it. But Ellen kept encouraging me.

It was during this time that Ellen revealed her desire to write about the 64-cube Snake puzzle. She was challenged with the question "How many solutions are there to the King Snake puzzle?" So here we are with her book.

In the book, you will see that there are many, many solutions to the King Snake Puzzle. Also, you will be exposed to the algorithms Ellen developed for getting the answers to her challenge. For those who love to solve puzzles and ponder the mathematics behind them, this is a delightful book. You will appreciate Ellen's love of puzzles.

Diane Minnix

Are you ready to embark on an intellectual odyssey like no other? Dive into the captivating world of "Pondering Solutions to the King Snake Puzzle, an adventure in Discrete Mathematics", a workbook that transcends the boundaries of traditional academia.

As you navigate the pages of this workbook, prepare to be immersed in a rich tapestry of knowledge. Flip back and forth between plain text pages, where the story of our adventure unfolds, and the extensive appendices and glossary, where the meat of mathematics awaits. Here you will find the tools and insights needed to conquer the King Snake Puzzle and emerge victorious.

Whether you are a seasoned mathematician or a curious novice, this book offers a unique and engaging learning experience.

D.S.

Thank You

Thanks to the following folks for their generous help and wise counsel while my adventurous experiment continued:

Bernard Grossholz
Susan Grossholz
Diane Minnix
Dana Scott
Linda Stoddard
Anne Whalen
Dr. Giray Okten

Table of Contents   Page

Table of Contents Page

King Snake
4x4x4 snake Puzzle
A VERY tough puzzle,
Pieces stay connected,
twisting all about. Can
you get them back to the
cube?
CreativeCrafthouse.com

There are 2 possible solutions to this puzzle. They are both shown in the tables below. To understand the code, think of each block in the snake as numbered from 1 to 64. Each group of numbers below represents how the blocks fit into the 4 levels of the cube. They are a roadmap of how to wind the snake to make the cube. For ex, **viewing Sol #1**; start with the end of the snake that has 3 blocks connected in a straight line (the first block is light colored) and begin to wrap the snake as shown on the top level. Note that after block #6, the snake starts to wind down into the 2nd level (the level below the top level). Blocks 7-11 are on the 2nd level, blocks 12-15 are positioned back on the top level, block 16 moves down to the 2nd level, block 17 starts the 3rd level down, etc....
Note that the odd numbers will all be light colored blocks and all even numbers dark blocks

		top Level				2nd Level				3rd Level				bottom level		
Sol #1	1	2	3	12	8	9	10	11	43	44	57	58	42	45	60	59
	6	5	4	13	7	32	31	30	34	33	56	55	41	46	61	54
	21	20	15	14	36	19	16	29	35	18	17	52	40	47	62	53
	22	23	26	27	37	24	25	28	38	49	50	51	39	48	63	64

		top Level				2nd Level				3rd Level				bottom level		
Sol #2	32	1	6	7	33	2	5	8	36	3	4	49	37	38	39	48
	31	22	15	14	34	21	20	9	35	54	53	50	56	55	40	47
	30	23	16	13	29	24	19	10	28	27	52	51	57	58	41	46
	63	64	17	12	62	25	18	11	61	26	43	44	60	59	42	45

Pondering Solutions to the King Snake Puzzle
An Adventure in Discrete Mathematics

1.0 The Challenge

The package from Amazon contained two copies of the 64-cube King Snake Puzzle along with an insert from Creative Crafthouse describing the puzzle. The challenge popped out at me within a half-hour after I opened the package.

I had put the two puzzles on my kitchen table facing each other in the manner shown in the picture on the opposite page. These **physical solutions** looked to be mirror-image solutions, two different solutions.

And, I had read the insert from Creative Crafthouse. A copy of the insert is also on the opposite page. The insert showed me two solutions with cube numbers in grids. They were two different **digital solutions**,

with cube sixty-four **in a corner of a grid** in solution number one and

cube sixty-four **next to a corner of a grid** in solution number two.

Perhaps one of the solutions sitting on my kitchen table was a rendering from digital solution number two on the insert? The physical solutions had the same beginnings as digital solution number two. i.e. with cube[64] in position next to the corner. But I couldn't figure it out. I couldn't see enough to compare the paths of the snakes through the two types of solutions, with one being a physical solution sitting on my table and one being a digital solution on the insert from Creative Crafthouse.

So, on my kitchen table I saw two different solutions. On the insert from Creative Crafthouse there were two different solutions. Was I looking at three, or was it four, different solutions? And the insert from Creative Crafthouse says, "There are two possible solutions to the puzzle." I interpreted that to mean, "There are only two solutions to the puzzle", and I saw at least three.

Then, I stretched out one of the physical puzzles on my dining room table. I stretched it as straight as it would straighten. That's what is shown in the picture on the front cover. I saw there were several bends in its path. To me, that suggested opportunity for many, many solutions – much more than three.

The question? The challenge? How many solutions are there to the King Snake Puzzle?

2.0 How to Read This Book

This discourse is a lab report, a workbook. It was written in a virtual laboratory behind a door labelled "Discrete Mathematics". As such its genre is "academic". This workbook is not to be scanned. It is to be examined and its lab reports verified in a similar laboratory where there is a general-purpose computer running Microsoft Excel and where there is a copy of the King Snake Puzzle of sixty-four wooden cubes in a 4x4x4 array.

Before you go any further, know this: I built a Microsoft Excel macro, coded in the programming language "Visual Basic", that generates digital solutions to the King Snake Puzzle. The name of the macro is "Harry". I talk about Harry's solutions or Harry's digital solutions. Harry has become a primary member of the cast of characters in my adventure towards answering the challenge.

As you study the pages of this workbook expect to be flipping back and forth among these plain-text pages, the many appendices, and the Glossary. The meat of the mathematics is in the glossary and the other appendices. The route of my adventure is in these plain-text pages.

2.1 About the Glossary and the Table of Contents

I've chosen words and terms to use with special meaning. I've also used a special syntax to make sentences and paragraphs precise but shorter. The words and the syntax are pictured, explained, or defined in the Glossary, the last appendix in this workbook. It's time now for you to look over the Glossary. Scan it to get an understanding of the kinds of things you might want to look up when you come across them in your reading. Below is a list of items to get familiar with NOW.

Coordinates of the 4x4x4 array
Position or poscode or pos
Octants
Ultimate Corner
Cube[n]
Names of the solutions
Digital Solution
Physical Solution
Visual Anchor

3.0 My Adventure

My adventure in discrete mathematics begins here. Enjoy.

3.1 The Back Story

A couple of years ago I bought a copy of the smaller snake puzzle, the one with twenty-seven cubes. When in a solved state, it sits in a 3x3x3 array of cubes. I wanted to know how to solve it, but I could see that solving it would take a lot of patience along with an ability to remember which paths had been tried and rejected. I had neither the patience nor the memory. So, instead of trying to solve it myself, I watched a video on YouTube showing a fellow solving the puzzle. I paused the video every now and then, backed it up, started forward again, and viewed his actions. Over and over I did that, making notes as I went.

Out of that came my published version of how to solve the 27-cube snake puzzle. It appears in Appendix 1. A list in the appendix shows a position in the 3x3x3 array for each of the twenty-seven cubes. The list is annotated with ten steps for a human to take in solving the puzzle. Yes, only ten steps for placing the twenty-seven cubes. Also, in the appendix there is a description of the "visual anchor" and its use in solving the puzzle.

I've had fun with that. I've shared the puzzle and my write-up with several friends and relatives. More than one of them said, "But there are no numbers on the cubes!" I responded, "That's right. You don't need numbers on the cubes. The next step places the next cubes."

You might have observed that the first steps to solving the puzzle do not place the first cubes. They do place several cubes, however, and among them are the visual anchor, cubes 7, 8, 9, and 10. I didn't need numbers on the cubes for that. I could count to ten.

3.2 Let me Introduce Eloise

I wanted to jump in and build Harry, but I wasn't quite ready. I planned to model his algorithm after what the human would do to solve the physical puzzle i.e., lay the next cube down in an available next place until there were no more available next places. Then back cubes out of place far enough back that the beginning of an alternate path forward becomes visible. I needed to find a way to test the algorithm before I built Harry. So, I built Eloise instead of Harry. Eloise is a Microsoft Excel macro that implements the model to generate a solution to the

27-cube snake puzzle. And Eloise's product is precisely the same solution as the one I copied from the YouTube video! My algorithm passed its first test.

3.3 Harry

Next, Harry came into existence. He successfully generated a solution to the 64-cube snake puzzle starting from the seeds cube[1] at position[111] and cube[2] at position[112]. I was delighted.

Right away, I needed to figure how to modify Harry so that he could generate more than one solution from a pair of seeds. It came to me. Change Harry so that when he successfully places cube[64], indicating that he has generated a solution, he asks himself "Is this the solution that I am to copy onto the Excel worksheet, or shall I look further?" And when the answer is to look further, he merely backs out cube[64] thereby beginning the search for another solution.

Appendix 6 contains a full description of Harry as well as a listing of his Visual Basic Code and his template.

3.4 How many Pairs of Seeds, How Many Solutions

I wanted to get a count of seeds for Harry – first, the count of seeds in octant[111]. So ... I sat down with my thinking cap in good shape and derived a list of all the pairs of positions for cube[1] and cube[2] in which at least one of the cubes was in octant[111]. In support to this analysis, I needed the nitty-gritty display that shows the eight positions in each of the eight octants of the 4x4x4 array, as in the chart that is in App2 page 2. I found thirty-six pairs of positions. I called them "candidate seeds."

Then came Margo. Margo is a Microsoft Excel macro that counts digital solutions. She is a modified version of Harry. Given a pair of candidate seeds and the command "Go", she runs and runs until she has generated every digital solution that can be generated from that candidate pair. Then, satisfied with her work, she writes the count on her Excel worksheet. I set Margo to work on each of the thirty-six pairs of candidate seeds.

See App2 page 3 for Margo's counts. The 36 pairs are listed in the chart sorted on the position of cube[1] in the pair. Margo gives us non-zero counts of solutions for only 6 of the 36 candidate pairs. Ergo, only six of the candidate pairs are pairs of **seeds** for Harry, seeds in Octant[111]. These are the positions for cube[1] & cube[2] in the seeds that Margo gives us:

111&112   **111**&121   **111**&211
112&**111**   121&**111**   211&**111**

I introduced classifications for these six pairs of seeds, Alpha Class and Beta Class. These Alpha class seeds have cube[1] in position[111] and the Beta class seeds have cube[2] in position**[111]**

Alpha Class	Beta Class
111&112	112&**111**
111&121	121&**111**
111&211	211&**111**

Still looking at App2 page 3, we see that Margo's data shows 2 digital solutions can be generated from each of the 3 alpha class pairs of seeds, and 6 digital solutions can be generated from each of the 3 beta class pairs of seeds. That's 6 alpha class plus 18 beta class. Ergo, Margo reports that from octant[111], Harry can generate 24 digital solutions from 6 pairs of seeds.

Switch to App2 page 4, "All Octants", and take an intuitive leap. This chart shows Margo's data extrapolated into each of the other seven octants. Margo's data for octant[111] are shown at the top of the chart, lines 1, 2, and 3.

Let me include a note here about extrapolating the positions for the alpha class cube[2] and the beta class cube[1]: Examine Margo's data, one line at a time. The difference between the positions for cube[1] and cube[2] in her first line? The difference is in the coordinate "row", in her second line the difference is in the coordinate "aisle", and in her third line the difference is in the coordinate "floor". The extrapolations were accomplished line by line from octant[111] to respective lines in each of the other seven octants.

The chart on App2 page 4 lists 24 pairs of seeds for alpha class and 24 pairs of seeds for beta class, 48 alpha class digital solutions, and 144 beta class digital solutions. For Harry, that's a grand total of 192 digital solutions.

One hundred ninety-two digital solutions! This is the answer to my Challenge!

But is it? I had to look at my challenge again. This is how I stated it at the beginning of my adventure on page 1: "How many *solutions* are there to the King

Snake Puzzle?" And now I'm talking about a count of 192 *digital solutions*. I had to add a challenge to my adventure as follows: "How many *physical solutions* are there to the King Snake Puzzle?"

The one hundred ninety-two lists that Harry generates are digital solutions and the solutions printed in the grids on the insert from Creative Crafthouse are digital solutions. [See *page viii* opposite page 1.] The physical solutions are the ones sitting on my kitchen table in a neat 4x4x4 array of wooden cubes fastened together by an elastic band. It's a long way from "there are one hundred ninety-two *digital solutions*" to "How many *physical solutions* are there to the King Snake Puzzle?" Hint: 192 divided by 24 equals 8.

[This topic is continued in "Section 3.8, From 192 Digital Solutions to a Count of Physical Solutions,"]

3.5 Let's Give a Look at Harry's Work

There are two listings for the solution[134&144 First] in the Appendix 3. The first listing is the one that Harry generates. In addition to the positions for each of the cubes, it contains data about Harry's neighbor arrays and his counts of backups.

As Harry attempts to place a <u>corner</u> cube[n] he tries to build the corner cube's neighbor array, an array containing the positions of all of the available spaces for cube[n+1]. A corner cube might have as many as four available spaces for cube[n+1]. When Harry finds that there are no spaces available for cube[n+1], he backs out cube[n]. This means that a space is always available for Harry to place cube[n+1] after corner cube[n] is successfully placed.

The data in the listing shows the state of the neighbor arrays after Harry successfully places cube[64]. Cube]58] sits in position[441] which was the second entry in the neighbor array for cube[57]. And cube[59] sits in position[341], the last entry in the neighbor array for cube[58].

As to the counts of backups: I am amazed. These counts are so big I am amazed that any human being can ever solve the King Snake Puzzle. Yes, Harry backs out cubes one at a time, and the human backs out segments. So what? It's going to be a large number of backups for the human, too. Harry keeps up with what to try next by building and using the neighbor arrays. Every time a corner cube is backed out, that corner cube will get a new neighbor array when it is again that corner cube's turn to be placed in the 4x4x4 array. How does the human keep up with all of that? It amazes me.

Let's look at my assertion that each of Harry's one hundred ninety-two digital solutions is a unique solution. I see from Margo's data showing the pairs of seeds in octant[111] that each pair is different from all the others. I add on to that. I see the way Harry builds more than one solution from a pair of seeds. The counts of backups are cumulative from solution to solution. Over and over again he builds NEW neighbor arrays. Harry doesn't try the old paths again. He tries NEW paths.

3.6 For the Puzzler with the Puzzle on His Hands

See the second listing in Appendix 3, Solution[134&144 First]. This is the list for "the puzzler with the puzzle on his hands." This is Harry's list of coordinates for each cube along with annotations instructing the human how to solve the puzzle. It describes twenty-six steps for placing the sixty-four cubes in the 4x4x4 array. From among Harry's one hundred ninety-two digital solutions, I chose solution[134&144 First] to be annotated for use by the human <u>because</u> I like to build floors from the bottom up. In the first nine steps, solution[134&144First] places twenty-two cubes in the 4x4x4 array and sixteen of them are in slab[Floor 1]. (Note: Solution 134&144 First] is entry #10 on App5 page 5.)

Some notes: The yellow cube numbers on the instructions highlight the eight cubes sitting in the ultimate corners of the 4x4x4 array. Coordinates for the straight cubes are shown in gray. To help in understanding the steps' instructions, some of the coordinate values are bolded. The bolding emphasizes the coordinate whose value is changing from cube to cube within the step.

But don't rush off. There are things to do before you set off to build a 4x4x4 array from your string of sixty-four wooden cubes.

Things to do for yourself: Study App 2 page 2, "Positions in the Octants of the 4x4x4 Array". Get familiar with reading the positions. Remember that "position[114]" is "position one one four" rather than "position one hundred fourteen". And you want to know, for instance, that position[114] is "bottom floor, leftmost aisle, rear row". Look up "Coordinates" in the Glossary, Appendix 7.

Things to do to the sixty-four wooden cubes: Stretch the snake out on your tabletop as straight as you can, with each cube sitting directly on the tabletop. Identify the end of the string that is to be cube[1] by comparing the makeup of cubes 1 through 5 to the **type of cube**, straight or corner, as listed in Harry's instructions. Then, locate cube[20]. It is to be your visual anchor. I marked my cube[20] with a bit of red sticky tape. Ink? Crayon? Fingernail polish? Mark it somehow so that it can be located easily.

How I use the visual anchor: I look at cube[20] sitting in position[111] and know that I am looking at the bottom floor, the leftmost aisle, the front row. When I read from the instructions that cube[2] is to be placed in position[144], that tells me the placement relative to the placement of cube[20]. Cube[2]'s place is on the same floor as cube[20], to the rightmost aisle away from cube[20], and in the rear row far behind cube[20].

I suggest that you re-position cube[20] to position[111] of the 4x4x4 array on the table in front of you in preparation for performing **each step** of the instructions. Use the visual anchor. There are no cube numbers on the cubes.

Be sure to begin with Step 1, not cube[1].

Now, go put your snake back into its cage.

3.7   The Digital Solutions from Creative Crafthouse.

After I got familiar with working slabs of sixteen spaces and slabs of sixteen cubes, I went back to study the insert from Creative Crafthouse. I wanted to know which of Harry's digital solutions were represented on the insert. The slabs are labelled "top level", "2nd Level", etc. on the insert. I easily interpreted "Level" to be Harry's "Floor". But what about the other two coordinates?

The answer to that question is in Appendix 4, "Creative Crafthouse Solutions".

In order to compare CC's solutions to Harry's, I had to reverse Harry's cube numbers. CC's cube[64] is Harry's cube[1]. And on CC's solution #2, I reversed the floor coordinate. I assigned both the aisle and row coordinates so that I could see a match to Harry's solution[111&121 First] and solution[121&111 Fourth]. They are one alpha class solution and one beta class solution.

Cube numbers in the slabs[Floor] shown on page 6 of Appendix 4 were lifted from Harry's solutions where I had reversed the cube numbers. They are the same as the cube numbers in "Levels" shown on the insert from Creative Crafthouse that is opposite page 1 of this workbook.

3.8 From 192 Digital Solutions to a Count of Physical Solutions

How many physical solutions are there? There are eight: two alpha class and six beta class.

The counts are evidenced in the data reported by Margo in App2 and repeated in App5 page 2, "Counts of Paths of Solution per Pair of Seeds, Alpha and Beta Class". The charts in the two appendices show the same numbers. Only the names of things are different. In App5 page 2, I included the word "family" here and there.

Look at Margo's data for the Beta class family in App5 page 2. The long column of sixes jumps out at me. Margo has a message for me in those twenty-four sixes: There are 24 beta class paths of solutions per beta class family and there are six beta class families. And regarding the alpha class data: There are 24 alpha class paths of solutions per alpha class family and there are two alpha class families.

Now look at App 5 page 3. Seeing the six charts for the beta class families on App 5 page 3 helps me see how the six solutions per pair of seeds are distributed in the families. For the beta class families, it takes six charts to place one hundred forty-four unique beta class paths of solution. That's six families, one family per chart.

And for the alpha class families, with two solutions per pair of seeds, the count is two families to place forty-eight unique paths of solution.

Two alpha class families plus six beta class families equals eight families. One family per physical solution? That's eight physical solutions.

To help in understanding, I've included the two charts on App5 page 4. They show the names of all twenty-four paths of solution in the first alpha class and the first beta class families. You'll see later how I arrived at the names. It wasn't easy.

3.8.1 There Are Eight Physical Solutions

Yes, "Eight" is the answer to my second challenge, but I was just not satisfied. My adventure continued with a third challenge. "What are the **names** of the twenty-four paths of solutions in each of the two alpha class physical solutions and in each of the six beta class physical solutions?" I had to remember it's one family per physical solution.

How could I collect those names? I had to get the names from Harry's digital solutions. How, how, how was that to be done?

3.8.2 Learning to Transpose a Digital Solution

I sat at my table with a beta class physical solution sitting in front of me on the table. The gizmo sat in its 4x4x4 array limited in its position by coordinates that oriented it to my understanding of the real world, namely coordinates floor, aisle, and row. I had put it in the array with seeds[112&111]. I picked up the gizmo, freeing it from its limits as to orientation. I turned it around, rotated it, flipped it, and put it down again this time with seeds[412&411]. I had not changed the positional relationships among the cubes within the gizmo. I had not shaken the thing like salt in a saltshaker. Each cube had the same neighbors after I put the gizmo down as it had had before I picked it up. It did not take me a long time. [See Margo's chart on App5 page 2.] I realized I could place the gizmo back in the 4x4x4 array with the seeds in **any one of the 24 positions** presented in Margo's chart for a beta class family of seeds.

I needed to examine what was happening to the positions of all of the cubes when I rotated the gizmo. Where were they going? How were their coordinates changing? I had built the physical solution in the first place from Harry's digital solution[112&111 First]. What was happening to that path of solution? I put the gizmo down on my table in the 4x4x4 array with seeds set again to [112&111] and rotated the gizmo toward me. It's the action that I now call "rotate slabs of aisle 90 degrees clockwise". The seeds moved to seeds[214&114] and the cubes in slabs[aisle] **remained** in slabs[aisle]. I saw it happen.

I moved to my computer to examine Excel worksheets. Two of the Excel worksheets I needed to examine are included in App5 pages 6-9. There you can see the slabs[Aisle] to be compared in a blue background. I compared

slabs[aisle] from . . . . .digital solution[112&111 First] to the **six slabs[aisle] from the six digital solutions** out of seeds[214&114].

I found that Slabs[aisle] from digital solution[112&111 First]

matched Slabs[aisle] from digital solution[214&114 Sixth] !!!!!

Sixth! I had found the ordinal number to go with the pair of seeds. I had identified the name of the rotationally equivalent digital solution. I had learned how to transpose a path of solution from one octant of origin to another. Or so I thought. I had not yet butted into "the frustrated transposition."

Note: This transposition is included in App5 page 5, the sixth entry.

3.9 Squeezing 192 Digital Solutions into 8 Physical Solutions

Too many thoughts were running through my head at the same time. Too many possibilities opened up. I had to stop. Make a plan. Pick a topic to address first. I picked "paths of rotation". (A look ahead: the chart on App 5 page 5 is a concise story of the whole of section 3.9. Keep it in mind as you study section 3.9 and its sub sections.)

3.9.1 Paths of Rotation

I had the names of two members in the family[112&111 First]. I had acquired the second one by rotating slabs[Aisle] 90 degrees clockwise from the first member. By observing possible rotations of the gizmo, I could see that nine paths of rotation were available from solution[112&111 First]. They are

Rotate slabs[Floor] 90 degrees clockwise

Rotate slabs[Floor] 90 degrees counterclockwise.

Rotate slabs[Floor] 180 degrees

Rotate slabs[Aisle] 90 degrees clockwise

Rotate slabs[Aisle] 90 degrees counterclockwise

Rotate slabs[Aisle] 180 degrees

Rotate slabs[Row] 90 degrees clockwise

Rotate slabs[Row] 90 degrees counterclockwise

Rotate slabs[Row] 180 degrees

I had eight more paths of rotation yet to apply. Eight more transpositions gave me a total of ten members of the family. [The nine members identified by transposing from solution[112&111 first] are shown in App5 page 5 where they are presented with a yellow background.]

After performing this first level of transposition there were still fourteen pairs of seeds without ordinal numbers, i.e., fourteen members of the family that were not yet fully identified .

What was the next topic in my plan?

3.9.2 Some Rules I Have Learned to Trust

Rules 1.a and 1.b and 1.c all mean the same thing.

(1.a) If digital solution A is rotationally equivalent to digital solution B then digital solution B is rotationally equivalent to digital solution A.

(1.b) If path of solution A transposes to path of solution B then path of solution B transposes to path of solution A.

(1.c) If solution A transposes to solution B then solution B transposes to solution A.

(2) If solution A transposes to solution B then solutions A and B are members of the same family of solutions.

(3) If solution A transposes to solution B and solution B transposes to solution C then solutions A, B, and C are members of the same family of solutions.

3.9.3 The Rest of The Plan

I took the nine members I identified in my first level of transposition, and then, in a second level of transposition, testing and trusting my rules, I got eighty-one identifications of solutions in the same family by applying each of the nine paths of rotation to each of the nine members identified in the first level of transposition.

Altogether, in the two levels of transposition, I performed ninety transpositions. App5 page 5, on the right hand side of the chart, shows the twenty-four members of the family along with the count of times each solution was identified as a member. I was pleased to see proof of rules 1.a and 1.b and 1.c in the big fat black **9** next to solution[112&111 First]. In accordance with the rules, Solution[112&111 First] was the object of nine transpositions in the second level of transpositions.

I was pleased to see that my rules 2 and 3 for identifying the twenty-four members of the family did the trick. (1) In the ninety transpositions, each of the members was identified at least three times. (2) In the ninety transpositions, ONLY the select twenty-four members were identified.

Also in the chart on App5 page 5, I included one of the paths of rotation to each member. I wanted to see how the rotational paths fit in the picture. Remember: The entries with the yellow background are the nine transpositions in the first level.

3.9.4 Getting Ready to Transpose Beta Class Solutions

To prepare for transposing digital solutions I had to generate a large beta class database. The database is made up of twenty-four Excel workbooks. That's one workbook for each pair of beta class seeds. The title of each workbook is the name of its pair of beta class seeds.

Each workbook contains at least nine worksheets.

There is one worksheet for each of the six digital solutions that Harry built from the titled pair of beta class seeds. In addition to showing Harry's coordinates per cube, the worksheet has three columns of cubes in slabs[Floor], slabs[Aisle], slabs[Row], derived from Harry's list of coordinates per cube.

Each workbook also contains three worksheets with lists of cubes in slabs. One of the three worksheets contains six lists of cubes[Floor]. That is one list from each of the six digital solutions in the workbook. The second of the three worksheets contains six lists of slabs[Aisle], and the third worksheet contains six lists of slabs[Row].

24 workbooks times 9 worksheets per workbook is 216 very expensive worksheets. But it's been fun.

3.9.5 The Frustrated Transpositions

There was a bump in the road in transposing the beta class digital solutions. I gave the bump a label. It frustrated me so I called it "frustrated transposition". Thirty of the ninety transpositions I performed were frustrated. Let me tell you about one of them.

I had chosen the transposition from solution[112&111 First] to solution[442&441 First], to transpose by rotating slabs[row] 180 degrees. The frustration occurred in performing the second step, in attempting to match slabs[row] from solution[112&111 First] to **one** of the six slabs[row] out of the six solutions generated from seeds[442&441]. See App5 pages 6-7 and 10-11, the slabs[Row] with the yellow background.

Slabs[Row] from **both** solution[442&441 **First**] and
slabs[Row] from . . . . .solution[442&441 **Fourth**] matched
slabs[Row] from . . . . .solution[112&111 First].`
Frustration, frustration! Which is it? First or Fourth?

3.9.6 Resolving a Frustrated Transposition

When I rotate a gizmo the coordinates of all of the cubes in all of its twenty-four solutions change. When I transpose by rotating slabs[Row] in solution[112&111 First] 180 degrees, cubes in slabs[Row] remain in slabs[Row] and cubes in slabs[Floor] move to slabs[Floor] inverted, i.e.,

Cubes in slab[Floor 1] move to slab[Floor 4],
Cubes in slab[Floor 2] move to slab[Floor 3],
Cubes in slab[Floor 3] move to slab[Floor 2], and
Cubes in slab[Floor 4] move to slab[Floor 1].

In order to resolve the frustrated transposition of my sample, I had to compare the list of cubes in **slabs[Floor] inverted** from solution[**112&111 First**] to both
list of cubes in **slabs[Floor] . . . .** from solution[**442&441 First**] and
list of cubes in **slabs[Floor] . . . .** from solution[**442&441 Fourth**].
The comparisons show a match to one and only one of the lists of slabs from solution[442&441]. In this sample, it is the list from **solution[442&441 First]** thereby resolving the frustration.

The slabs[Floor] are shown in pink on App5 pages 6-7 and 12-13. This transposition appears in the chart on App5 page 5, entry 19.

A similar route exists for resolving a frustration resulting from transposing via each of the other eight paths of rotation.

3.9.7 Alpha Class Physical Solutions

There are two alpha class physical solutions. Together their families include the names of 48 solutions. I performed the first phase of the required transpositions to get the coordinates of the seeds of the solutions using a physical solution that I had put together following one of Harry's lists. I performed the second phase to obtain the ordinal numbers for completing the names of the solutions by working with pencil on quadrille paper.

Working with the alpha class did not prepare me for the difficulties of the frustrated transpositions of the beta class.

4.0 About My Third Challenge

In section 3.8.1 I stated a third challenge: "What are the names of the twenty-four solutions in each of the alpha class physical solutions and in each of the beta class physical solutions?" When I realized so much work was required (6 more families times 90 transpositions per family), I chose to reduce my challenge to match the answers I already had and to allow myself another intuitive leap into the additional six families.

I reduced the challenge to: "What are the names of the twenty-four solutions in the first alpha class physical solution and in the first beta class physical solution?" These names are shown in App5 page 4.

5.0   Finale, Digital vs. Physical

At the beginning of my adventure, early in 2021, shortly after I received my first two copies of the King Snake Puzzle, when my first challenge was forming in my mind, I chose the words "digital" and "physical" for the two types of solutions represented on page *viii*: "digital" being a presentation of numbers in a chart and "physical" being 64 little wooden cubes in a neat stack in a 4x4x4 array.

In an e-mail from Dr. Giray Okten, Mathematics Department, Florida State University, Professor Okten stated "I am afraid I have not understood the distinction between digital and physical solutions. When I first read page *viii* and page 1, I thought a digital solution is a representation of a physical solution using tables and diagrams." Your understanding is correct, Dr. Okten, but there is more, much more.

In May, 2024, now that I am at the end of the adventure in my virtual laboratory of discrete mathematics, I can report distinction between the two types of solutions. Digital: Each of the 192 unique digital solutions presents one and only one path of solution for the King Snake Puzzle. Physical: Each of the eight physical solutions incorporates a select twenty-four paths of solution out of the 192 digital solutions. And another way to put it, each of the eight physical solutions embodies a family of 24 digital solutions.

Such is the mystery of the King Snake Puzzle.

Appendix 1
The 27-Cube Snake Puzzle

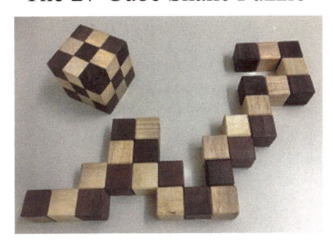

See Section 3.1 "The Back Story".

First Steps to Solving the Snake Cube Puzzle

The **Snake** is a string of twenty-seven cubes connected in sequence like beads on a string. The **Snake Cube** is a 3x3x3 array of those twenty-seven cubes. Solving the Snake Cube puzzle calls for placing the cubes, without breaking the string, into that 3x3x3 array.

Think of the 3x3x3 array of cubes as three **floors** with each floor having a 3x3 array of cubes. Picture the 3x3 array on each floor as **aisles** and **rows** like desks in a school room.

Let the floors be labelled 1st, 2nd, and 3rd ranging from bottom to top.
Let the aisles be labelled left, center, and right.
Let the rows be labelled front, middle, and back.

The chart on pages 4 and 5 shows the twenty-seven cubes identified by
(1) their sequence numbers on the string and (2) their positions in the 3x3x3 array of the solution. The positions have names of the form (Floor, Aisle, Row). Example: Position(3rd, Center, Middle) means (3rd Floor, Center Aisle, Middle Row). Primarily, the chart shows the sequence of the steps to solution.

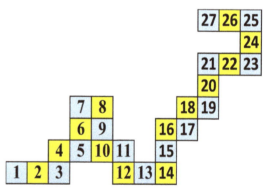

Begin: On a tabletop, spread out your puzzle in the pattern shown on the right. Place all twenty-seven cubes flat on the tabletop. Note: The numbers on the cubes in the pattern are the numbers on the cubes in both the drawing of the visual anchor on page 3 and in the chart on pages 4 and 5 that shows the steps to solution.

About cubes 5 through 10: In laying the cubes flat on the tabletop you got a head start on both the first and the second steps to solution. You left cubes 5 through 10 lying together flat on the tabletop. The first and second steps in the chart on page 4 say that next these six cubes are to stand upright in columns.

Look at the chart on page 4. See the descriptions for the first and second steps. Perform both the first and second steps now: With your left hand, hold cubes 4 and 11 flat to the tabletop and with your right hand turn cubes 5 through 10 upright so they look like columns. Cubes 7 and 8 become your visual anchor.

The Visual Anchor

In performing steps 1 and 2, you placed cubes 7 and 8 into positions
(3rd Floor, **Center Aisle**, Middle Row) and (3rd Floor, **Right Aisle**, Middle Row).
You established your visual anchor.

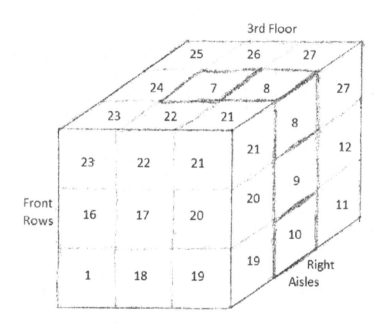

As you wrap the other cubes around to form the 3x3x3 array, use the two columns as a
visual anchor to keep your thinking oriented to the positions specified on the chart. For
example, look at the third step on the chart. The column titled "Row" shows that cube 4
goes in the back behind cube 5.

Go. Execute the third through the tenth steps. Solve the Snake Cube Puzzle.

Steps to Solving the Snake Cube Puzzle

Tint	Cube Name	Sequence of Steps	Position in the Snake Cube	Position in the 3x3x3 Array			Type of Cube	Cube Name	Tint
				Floor	Aisle	Row			
Dark	1	fourth	cubes on the 1st floor, **entire** left aisle	1st	left	front	Straight	1	Dark
Light	2			1st	left	middle	Straight	2	Light
Dark	3			1st	left	back	Corner	3	Dark
Light	4	third	1st floor, center aisle, cube in the back row.	1st	center	back	Corner	4	Light
Dark	5	**second**	cubes in a **column**, center aisle, middle row (This is the center column of all 9 columns.)	1st	center	middle	Corner	5	Dark
Light	6			2nd	center	middle	Straight	6	Light
Dark	7			3rd	center	middle	Corner	7	Dark
Light	8	**first**	cubes in a **column**, right aisle, middle row	3rd	right	middle	Corner	8	Light
Dark	9			2nd	right	middle	Straight	9	Dark
Light	10			1st	right	middle	Corner	10	Light
Dark	11	fifth	1st floor, right aisle, cube in the back row.	1st	right	back	Corner	11	Dark
Light	12	sixth	cubes on the 2nd floor: **entire** back row, and **entire** left aisle	2nd	right	back	Corner	12	Light
Dark	13			2nd	center	back	Straight	13	Dark
Light	14			2nd	left	back	Corner	14	Light
Dark	15	seventh		2nd	left	middle	Straight	15	Dark
Light	16			2nd	left	front	Corner	16	Light
Dark	17	eighth	cubes stacked on the 1st and 2nd floors, center aisle, front row	2nd	center	front	Corner	17	Dark
Light	18			1st	center	front	Corner	18	Light

Steps to Solving the Snake Cube Puzzle

Tint	Cube Name	Sequence of Steps	Position in the Snake Cube	Position in the 3x3x3 Array			Type of Cube	Cube Name	Tint
				Floor	Aisle	Row			
Dark	19	ninth	cubes in a **column**, right aisle, front row	1st	right	front	Corner	19	Dark
Light	20			2nd	right	front	Straight	20	Light
Dark	21			3rd	right	front	Corner	21	Dark
Light	22	tenth	cubes on the 3rd floor: **entire** front row, **entire** left aisle, and **entire** back row	3rd	center	front	Straight	22	Light
Dark	23			3rd	left	front	Corner	23	Dark
Light	24			3rd	left	middle	Straight	24	Light
Dark	25			3rd	left	back	Corner	25	Dark
Light	26			3rd	center	back	Straight	26	Light
Dark	27			3rd	right	back	Straight	27	Dark

...

Appendix 2

Seeds, Counts of Solutions, and Octants

See Section 3.4 "How many Pairs of Seeds, How Many Solutions"

Octant[444] upper, right, rear

434	444
433	443

334	344
333	343

Octant[414] upper, left, rear

424	414
413	423

314	324
313	323

lower, right, rear Octant[144]

234	244
233	243

134	144
133	143

lower, left, rear Octant[114]

224	214
213	223

114	124
113	123

Octant[441] upper, right, front

432	442
431	441

332	342
331	341

lower, right, front Octant[141]

242	232
231	241

132	142
131	141

Octant[411] upper, left, front

412	422
411	421

312	322
311	321

lower, left, front Octant[111]

212	222
211	221

112	122
111	121

Positions in the Octants of the 4x4x4 Array

Positions of the eight ultimate corners of the array are **bolded**.

Appendix 2   Page 2

Octant 111, Tests for Seeds and Counts of Solutions

#	Candidate Pair of Seeds		Count of Solutions	#	Candidate Pair of Seeds		Count of Solutions
	Position for Cube[1]	Position for Cube[2]			Position for Cube[1]	Position for Cube[2]	
1	111	112	2	19	211	221	0
2	111	121	2	20	211	311	0
3	111	211	2	21	212	112	0
4	112	111	6	22	212	211	0
5	112	113	0	23	212	213	0
6	112	122	0	24	212	222	0
7	112	212	0	25	212	312	0
8	121	111	6	26	221	121	0
9	121	122	0	27	221	211	0
10	121	131	0	28	221	222	0
11	121	221	0	29	221	231	0
12	122	112	0	30	221	321	0
13	122	121	0	31	222	122	0
14	122	123	0	32	222	212	0
15	122	132	0	33	222	221	0
16	122	222	0	34	222	223	0
17	211	111	6	35	222	232	0
18	211	212	0	36	222	322	0

	All Octants, Forty-Eight Pairs of Seeds, Counts of Solutions				
	Alpha Class		Name of the Octant	**Beta Class**	
	Positions of the Seeds, Cube[1] & Cube[2]	Count of Solutions Generated from the Seeds	and Position of the Ultimate Corner	Positions of the Seeds, Cube[1] & Cube[2]	Count of Solutions Generated from the Seeds
1	111&112	2	**111**	112&111	6
2	111&121	2		121&111	6
3	111&211	2		211&111	6
4	114&113	2	**114**	113&114	6
5	114&124	2		124&114	6
6	114&214	2		214&114	6
7	141&142	2	**141**	142&141	6
8	141&131	2		131&141	6
9	141&241	2		241&141	6
10	144&143	2	**144**	143&144	6
11	144&134	2		134&144	6
12	144&244	2		244&144	6
13	411&412	2	**411**	412&411	6
14	411&421	2		421&411	6
15	411&311	2		311&411	6
16	414&413	2	**414**	413&414	6
17	414&424	2		424&414	6
18	414&314	2		314&414	6
19	441&442	2	**441**	442&441	6
20	441&431	2		431&441	6
21	441&341	2		341&441	6
22	444&443	2	**444**	443&444	6
23	444&434	2		434&444	6
24	444&344	2		344&444	6
	Total ==>	**48**		Total ==>	**144**

Appendix 3
Solution[134&144 First]

Harry's List, Solution[134&144 First]
Steps for Solving the King Snake Puzzle

See Section 3.5 "Let's Give a Look at Harry's Work"
See Section 3.6 "For the Puzzler with the Puzzle on His Hands"
See Appendix 6 "All About Harry"

Harry's List, Solution[134&144 First]

Tint	Cube Number, i.e. ==> n	Floor	Aisle	Row	Position Code	Type of Cube	Count of available neighbors	Neighbors of Cube(n) 1	2	3	4	Count of Backups begun from n	Count of Backups returned to n	Cube Number, i.e. ==> n
Dark	1	1	3	4	134	Straight								1
Light	2	1	4	4	144	Corner	1	244						2
Dark	3	1	4	3	143	Straight								3
Light	4	1	4	2	142	Straight								4
Dark	5	1	4	1	141	Corner	1	241						5
Light	6	1	3	1	131	Corner	0						1	6
Dark	7	2	3	1	231	Corner	2	241	221				1	7
Light	8	2	3	2	232	Corner	3	332	132	242			5	8
Dark	9	2	2	2	222	Corner	2	322	122				17	9
Light	10	2	2	3	223	Corner	2	323	123				50	10
Dark	11	2	3	3	233	Corner	1	333					145	11
Light	12	1	3	3	133	Corner	1	123				2	391	12
Dark	13	1	3	2	132	Corner	0					3	1,025	13
Light	14	1	2	2	122	Corner	0					17	2,596	14
Dark	15	1	2	3	123	Straight								15
Light	16	1	2	4	124	Corner	1	224				1,885	4,170	16
Dark	17	1	1	4	114	Corner	1	214				52	10,134	17
Light	18	1	1	3	113	Straight								18
Dark	19	1	1	2	112	Straight	1	211				7,852		19
Light	20	1	1	1	111	Corner	1	211				4,408	7,237	20
Dark	21	1	2	1	121	Corner	0					261	12,915	21
Light	22	2	2	1	221	Corner	0					453	26,267	22
Dark	23	2	1	1	211	Corner	1	311				1,086	68,330	23
Light	24	2	1	2	212	Straight								24
Dark	25	2	1	3	213	Straight						58,557		25
Light	26	2	1	4	214	Corner	0					38,057	26,282	26
Dark	27	3	1	4	314	Straight								27
Light	28	4	1	4	414	Corner	1	424				24,349	21,696	28
Dark	29	4	1	3	413	Corner	0					1,300	42,974	29
Light	30	3	1	3	313	Corner	0					3,146	84,418	30

#	Total A	Total B	Route A	Route B	Count	Type	Code				#	Shade
31	208,107	4,115			0	Corner	323	3	2	3	31	Dark
32	340,635	17,578		433	1	Corner	423	3	2	4	32	Light
33	651,580	43,271			0	Corner	424	4	2	4	33	Dark
34						Straight	324	4	2	3	34	Light
35	461,365	849,632			0	Corner	224	4	2	2	35	Dark
36						Straight	234	4	3	2	36	Light
37	226,427	590,619			0	Corner	244	4	4	2	37	Dark
38	407,081	34,524			0	Corner	344	4	4	3	38	Light
39	583,302	124,297			0	Corner	334	4	3	3	39	Dark
40	1,059,739	126,301			0	Corner	434	4	3	4	40	Light
41	1,364,643	270,871			0	Corner	444	4	4	4	41	Dark
42	1,713,189	535,721		343	1	Corner	443	3	4	4	42	Light
43	2,297,247	858,251		343	0	Corner	433	3	3	4	43	Dark
44	2,834,290	1,053,900		432	1	Corner	333	3	3	3	44	Light
45	3,550,592	1,474,788	342		2	Corner	332	2	3	3	45	Dark
46						Straight	322	2	2	3	46	Light
47	1,008,530	7,856,665		412	1	Corner	312	2	1	3	47	Dark
48	1,096,976	625,725		411	1	Corner	311	1	1	3	48	Light
49						Straight	321	1	2	3	49	Dark
50	117,375	2,970,421		441	0	Corner	331	1	3	3	50	Light
51	207,402	149,586			1	Corner	431	1	3	4	51	Dark
52						Straight	421	1	2	4	52	Light
53	12,885	617,782			0	Corner	411	1	1	4	53	Dark
54	14,303	37,650			0	Corner	412	2	1	4	54	Light
55						Straight	422	2	2	4	55	Dark
56		56,957		342		Straight	432	2	3	4	56	Light
57	504	21,923			1	Corner	442	2	4	4	57	Dark
58	56	1,912			0	Corner	441	1	4	4	58	Light
59	63	435			0	Corner	341	1	4	3	59	Dark
60						Straight	342	2	4	3	60	Light
61	4	578			0	Corner	343	3	4	3	61	Dark
62		19			0	Corner	243	3	4	2	62	Light
63						Straight	242	2	4	2	63	Dark
64						Straight	241	1	4	2	64	Light

Totals 18,464,949 18,464,949

STEPS FOR SOLVING THE KING SNAKE PUZZLE
Solution[134&144 First]

Tint	Type of Cube	Floor	Aisle	Row	Cube Number	Step Number	Instruction
Dark	Straight	1	3	4	1	8	Bottom floor, 3rd aisle, rear row
Light	Corner	1	4	4	2		Fill the rightmost aisle on the bottom floor.
Dark	Straight	1	4	3	3	7	
Light	Straight	1	4	2	4		
Dark	Corner	1	4	1	5		
Light	Corner	1	3	1	6	6	Form a short stack in the 1st and 2nd floors; the 3rd aisle and front row.
Dark	Corner	2	3	1	7		
Light	Corner	2	3	2	8	5	2nd floor, 2nd row, aisles 2 and 3
Dark	Corner	2	2	2	9		
Light	Corner	2	2	3	10	4	2nd floor, 3rd row, aisles 2 and 3
Dark	Corner	2	3	3	11		
Light	Corner	1	3	3	12	3	1st floor, 3rd aisle, rows 2 and 3
Dark	Corner	1	3	2	13		
Light	Corner	1	2	2	14	Step 2	Cubes 14-16 lie on the 1st floor. They lie in the 2nd aisle across rows 2, 3, and 4.
Dark	Straight	1	2	3	15		
Light	Corner	1	2	4	16		
Dark	Corner	1	1	4	17	Step 1	Place cubes 17, 18, 19, and 20 on the 1st floor. Fill the leftmost aisle, i. e. aisle 1. [Cube 20 is the **visual anchor**. Bottom floor, leftmost aisle, front row.]
Light	Straight	1	1	3	18		
Dark	Straight	1	1	2	19		
Light	Corner	1	1	1	20		
Dark	Corner	1	2	1	21	9	Cubes 21 - 22 form a short stack on the 1st and 2nd floors; in aisle 2 and row 1.
Light	Corner	2	2	1	22		
Dark	Corner	2	1	1	23	10	Step 10: Fill the leftmost aisle on the 2nd floor.
Light	Straight	2	1	2	24		
Dark	Straight	2	1	3	25		Notice: Cube 26 is positioned in both steps.
Light	Corner	2	1	4	26	11	Step 11: Form a short stack on floors 2, 3 and 4 in the leftmost aisle, the rear row.
Dark	Straight	3	1	4	27		
Light	Corner	4	1	4	28		
Dark	Corner	4	1	3	29	12	Form a short stack on floors 4 and 3; in the 1st aisle and 3rd row.
Light	Corner	3	1	3	30		
Dark	Corner	3	2	3	31	13	Form a short stack on floors 3 and 4; in the 2nd aisle and 3rd row.
Light	Corner	4	2	3	32		

STEPS FOR SOLVING THE KING SNAKE PUZZLE

Tint	Type of Cube	Position in the 4x4x4 Array			Cube Number	Step Number	Solution[134&144 First]
		Floor	Aisle	Row			
Dark	Corner	4	2	4	33	14	Form a short stack on floors 4 and 3; in the 2nd aisle and 4th row.
Light	Straight	3	2	4	34		
Dark	Corner	2	2	4	35	15	2nd floor, back row, aisles 2, 3, and 4.
Light	Straight	2	3	4	36		
Dark	Corner	2	4	4	37		
Light	Corner	3	4	4	38	16	3rd floor, back row, aisles 3 and 4.
Dark	Corner	3	3	4	39		
Light	Corner	4	3	4	40	17	Top floor, back row, aisles 3 and 4
Dark	Corner	4	4	4	41		
Light	Corner	4	4	3	42	18	Top floor, 3rd row, aisles 3 and 4
Dark	Corner	4	3	3	43		
Light	Corner	3	3	3	44	19	Step 19: Place cubes 44 and 45 on the 3rd floor, the 3rd aisle, across rows 2 and 3. Step 20: With cube 45 already set, place cubes 45-47 on the 3rd floor, the 2nd row, across aisles 1, 2, and 3.
Dark	Corner	3	3	2	45		
Light	Straight	3	2	2	46	20	
Dark	Corner	3	1	2	47		
Light	Corner	3	1	1	48	21	3rd floor, front row, aisles 1, 2, and 3.
Dark	Straight	3	2	1	49		
Light	Corner	3	3	1	50		
Light	Corner	4	3	1	51	22	4th floor, front row, aisles 1, 2, and 3.
Light	Straight	4	2	1	52		
Dark	Corner	4	1	1	53		
Light	Corner	4	1	2	54	23	4th floor, fill the second row.
Dark	Straight	4	2	2	55		
Light	Straight	4	3	2	56		
Dark	Corner	4	4	2	57		
Light	Corner	4	4	1	58	24	4th floor, rightmost aisle, front row.
Dark	Corner	3	4	1	59	25	3rd floor, rightmost aisle, rows 1, 2, and 3
Light	Straight	3	4	2	60		
Dark	Corner	3	4	3	61		
Light	Corner	2	4	3	62	26	2nd floor, rightmost aisle, rows 1, 2, and 3
Dark	Straight	2	4	2	63		
Light	Straight	2	4	1	64		

Appendix 4

Creative Crafthouse Solutions

CC's Solution #1, Solution 111 and 121 First   App 4 Page 2

CC's Solution #2, Solution 121 and 111 Fourth   App 4 Page 4

Solutions from Creative Crafthouse   App 4 Page 6

   Translated to Harry's Solutions

See Section 3.7 "The Digital Solutions from Creative Crafthouse"

CC's Solution #1, Solution 111 & 121 First   August 20, 2021   Solution 111 & 121 First

Tint	Cube's Seq. No. (n)	Floor	Aisle	Row	Position Code	Type of Cube	Count of Available Neighbors	Avail. Neighbor 1	Avail. Neighbor 2	Avail. Neighbor 3	Avail. Neighbor 4	Count of Backups Begun at n	Count of Backups Returned to n	Cube's Seq. No. (n)
Dark	1	1	1	1	111	Straight	1	221						1
Light	2	1	2	1	121	Corner								2
Dark	3	1	2	2	122	Straight								3
Light	4	1	2	3	123	Straight								4
Dark	5	1	2	4	124	Corner	2	224	134					5
Light	6	1	1	4	114	Corner	0						1	6
Dark	7	2	1	4	214	Corner	0						1	7
Light	8	2	2	4	224	Corner	1	324					4	8
Dark	9	2	2	3	223	Corner	2	323	233				9	9
Light	10	2	1	3	213	Corner	1	313				1	26	10
Dark	11	1	1	3	113	Corner	0						87	11
Light	12	1	1	2	112	Corner	0					1	258	12
Dark	13	2	1	2	212	Corner	1	222				3	708	13
Light	14	2	1	1	211	Corner	1	311				9	1,837	14
Dark	15	2	2	1	221	Straight								15
Light	16	2	3	1	231	Corner	1	331				1,324	3,008	16
Dark	17	1	3	1	131	Corner	1	141				24	7,328	17
Light	18	1	3	2	132	Straight								18
Dark	19	1	3	3	133	Straight						5,572		19
Light	20	1	3	4	134	Corner	0					3,354	4,967	20
Dark	21	2	3	4	234	Corner	0					173	8,620	21
Light	22	2	4	4	244	Corner	1	344				230	17,864	22
Dark	23	1	4	4	144	Corner	0					735	46,302	23
Light	24	1	4	3	143	Straight						39,715		24
Dark	25	1	4	2	142	Straight								25
Light	26	1	4	1	141	Corner	0					25,657	19,168	26
Dark	27	2	4	1	241	Straight								27
Light	28	3	4	1	341	Corner	1	331				17,950	14,373	28
Dark	29	3	4	2	342	Corner	1	442				855	28,901	29
Light	30	2	4	2	242	Corner	1	232				2,112	58,181	30
Dark	31	2	4	3	243	Corner	1	343				3,071	140,390	31

Color	No.				Code	Type	n					No.
Light	32	2	3	3	233	Corner	0			8,716	235,365	32
Dark	33	3	3	3	333	Corner	1	343		26,503	439,723	33
Light	34	3	2	3	323	Straight						34
Dark	35	3	1	3	313	Corner	2	413	314	585,865	317,011	35
Light	36	3	1	2	312	Straight						36
Dark	37	3	1	1	311	Corner	0			421,145	151,844	37
Light	38	4	1	1	411	Corner	0			18,846	284,252	38
Dark	39	4	2	1	421	Corner	0			79,156	405,147	39
Light	40	3	2	1	321	Corner	0			72,020	742,702	40
Dark	41	3	3	1	331	Corner	0			180,963	921,064	41
Light	42	4	3	1	431	Corner	0			363,206	1,155,069	42
Dark	43	4	4	1	441	Corner	0			590,919	1,528,985	43
Light	44	4	4	2	442	Corner	0			659,864	1,977,587	44
Dark	45	4	3	2	432	Corner	0			988,469	2,383,222	45
Light	46	3	3	2	332	Straight						46
Dark	47	2	3	2	232	Corner	0			5,496,871	621,154	47
Light	48	2	2	2	222	Corner	0			343,379	749,962	48
Dark	49	3	2	2	322	Straight						49
Light	50	4	2	2	422	Corner	0			2,028,203	64,928	50
Dark	51	4	1	2	412	Corner	0			84,386	125,101	51
Light	52	4	1	3	413	Straight						52
Dark	53	4	1	4	414	Corner	0			363,174	5,672	53
Light	54	3	1	4	314	Corner	0			16,437	7,744	54
Dark	55	3	2	4	324	Straight						55
Light	56	3	3	4	334	Straight				29,543		56
Dark	57	3	4	4	344	Corner	1	444		9,118	321	57
Light	58	3	4	3	343	Corner	0			741	31	58
Dark	59	4	4	3	443	Corner	0			240	18	59
Light	60	4	3	3	433	Straight						60
Dark	61	4	2	3	423	Corner	0			384		61
Light	62	4	2	4	424	Corner	0			1		62
Dark	63	4	3	4	434	Straight						63
Light	64	4	4	4	444	Straight						64

Count of Backups ==> 12,468,935   12,468,935

CC's Solution #2, Solution 121 & 111 Fourth

August 15, 2021　　　Solution 121 & 111 Fourth

Tint	Cube's Sequence Number	Floor	Aisle	Row	Position Code	Type of Cube	Count of Available Neighbors	Avail. Neighbors 1	2	3	4	Count of Backups Begun	Count of Backups Returned	Cube's Sequence Number
Dark	1	1	2	1	121	Straight								1
Light	2	1	1	1	111	Corner	0						1	2
Dark	3	2	1	1	211	Straight								3
Light	4	3	1	1	311	Straight								4
Dark	5	4	1	1	411	Corner	0						2	5
Light	6	4	2	1	421	Corner	1	321					3	6
Dark	7	4	2	2	422	Corner	2	322	432				9	7
Light	8	4	1	2	412	Corner	1	312					33	8
Dark	9	4	1	3	413	Corner	1	313					99	9
Light	10	4	2	3	423	Corner	0						309	10
Dark	11	3	2	3	323	Corner	0						913	11
Light	12	3	3	3	333	Corner	3	433	233	334		5	2,457	12
Dark	13	3	3	2	332	Corner	2	432	232			27	6,555	13
Light	14	3	4	2	342	Corner	2	442	242			78	16,266	14
Dark	15	3	4	3	343	Straight	0					11,751	26,448	15
Light	16	3	4	4	344	Corner	0					301	64,959	16
Dark	17	4	4	4	444	Corner	1	434						17
Light	18	4	4	3	443	Straight	0					51,079		18
Dark	19	4	4	2	442	Straight	0					28,055		19
Light	20	4	4	1	441	Corner	0					1,393	45,317	20
Dark	21	3	4	1	341	Corner	0					2,310	80,954	21
Light	22	3	3	1	331	Corner	0					6,479	162,429	22
Dark	23	4	3	1	431	Corner	0						428,242	23
Light	24	4	3	2	432	Straight						373,974		24
Dark	25	4	3	3	433	Straight						233,693		25
Light	26	4	3	4	434	Corner	1	334					160,770	26
Dark	27	4	2	4	424	Straight						152,894		27
Light	28	4	1	4	414	Corner	0						126,943	28
Dark	29	3	1	4	314	Corner	1	324				6,816	264,252	29
Light	30	3	1	3	313	Corner	0					18,334	510,185	30
Dark	31	2	1	3	213	Corner	1	223				23,282	1,270,975	31
Light	32	2	1	4	214	Corner	0					98,620	2,035,041	32

	#	P1	P2	P3	Code	Type	Val	Ref1	Ref2	Backup A	Backup B	#
Dark	33	1	1	4	114	Corner	1	124		257,836	3,945,254	33
Light	34	1	1	3	113	Straight						34
Dark	35	1	1	2	112	Corner	0			5,201,696	2,736,635	35
Light	36	2	1	2	212	Straight						36
Dark	37	3	1	2	312	Corner	0			3,573,083	1,287,212	37
Light	38	3	2	2	322	Corner	1	222		193,195	2,243,175	38
Dark	39	3	2	1	321	Corner	0			681,208	3,284,941	39
Light	40	2	2	1	221	Corner	1	231		682,819	5,743,245	40
Dark	41	2	2	2	222	Corner	0			1,506,096	7,560,069	41
Light	42	1	2	2	122	Corner	1	132		2,962,930	9,225,776	42
Dark	43	1	2	3	123	Corner	0			4,462,781	12,948,718	43
Light	44	2	2	3	223	Corner	0			5,845,940	15,470,823	44
Dark	45	2	3	3	233	Corner	2	133	234	7,795,092	20,225,109	45
Light	46	2	3	2	232	Straight						46
Dark	47	2	3	1	231	Corner	0			44,184,645	5,804,217	47
Light	48	1	3	1	131	Corner	1	141		3,594,769	6,203,491	48
Dark	49	1	3	2	132	Straight						49
Light	50	1	3	3	133	Corner	0			16,806,733	705,890	50
Dark	51	1	4	3	143	Corner	2	243	144	805,299	1,310,654	51
Light	52	1	4	2	142	Straight						52
Dark	53	1	4	1	141	Corner	0			3,784,189	80,689	53
Light	54	2	4	1	241	Corner	0			221,823	90,653	54
Dark	55	2	4	2	242	Straight						55
Light	56	2	4	3	243	Straight				353,000		56
Dark	57	2	4	4	244	Corner	0			129,350	4,650	57
Light	58	1	4	4	144	Corner	0			14,276	725	58
Dark	59	1	3	4	134	Corner	0			3,699	423	59
Light	60	2	3	4	234	Straight						60
Dark	61	3	3	4	334	Corner	0			5,795	22	61
Light	62	3	2	4	324	Corner	0			165		62
Dark	63	2	2	4	224	Straight				23		63
Light	64	1	2	4	124	Straight						64

Count of Backups ==>   104,075,533   104,075,533

Solutions from Creative Crafthouse Translated to Harry's Solutions

****

Solution #1 from Creative Crafthouse with coordinates assigned to place **cube[64]** in Harry's **position[111]**.

CC Solution #1

Slab of **Floor 4**

Row				
4	1	2	3	12
3	6	5	4	13
2	21	20	15	14
1	22	23	26	27
Aisle	4	3	2	1

Slab of **Floor 3**

Row				
4	8	9	10	11
3	7	32	31	30
2	36	19	16	29
1	37	24	25	28
Aisle	4	3	2	1

Slab of **Floor 2**

Row				
4	43	44	57	58
3	34	33	56	55
2	35	18	17	52
1	38	49	50	51
Aisle	4	3	2	1

Slab of **Floor 1**

Row				
4	42	45	60	59
3	41	46	61	54
2	40	47	62	53
1	39	48	63	64
Aisle	4	3	2	1

With this assignment of coordinates, CC Solution #1 is Harry's Solution[111&121 First], an Alpha-Class solution.

****

Solution #2 from Creative Crafthouse with coordinates assigned to place **cube[64]** in Harry's **position[121]**.

CC Solution #2

Slab of **Floor 1**

Row				
4	32	1	6	7
3	31	22	15	14
2	30	23	16	13
1	63	64	17	12
Aisle	4	3	2	1

Slab of **Floor 2**

Row				
4	33	2	5	8
3	34	21	20	9
2	29	24	19	10
1	62	25	18	11
Aisle	4	3	2	1

Slab of **Floor 3**

Row				
4	36	3	4	49
3	35	54	53	50
2	28	27	52	51
1	61	26	43	44
Aisle	4	3	2	1

Slab of **Floor 4**

Row				
4	37	38	39	48
3	56	55	40	47
2	57	58	41	46
1	60	59	42	45
Aisle	4	3	2	1

With this assignment of coordinates, CC Solution #2 is Harry's Solution[121&111 Fourth], a Beta-Class solution.

Appendix 4   Page 6

Appendix 5

From One Hundred Ninety-Two Digital Solutions to Eight Physical Solutions

See Section 3.8 "From 192 Digital Solutions to a Count of Physical Solutions"

See Section 3.9 "Squeezing 192 Digital Solutions into 8 Physical Solutions"

See Appendix 3 "Solution[134&144 First]"

Counts of Paths of Solution per Pair of Seeds, Alpha and Beta Class

#	Alpha Class Family Positions of the Seeds, Cube[1] & Cube[2]	Count of Alpha Class Paths of Solutions Generated from the Seeds	Name of the Octant and Position of the Ultimate Corner	Beta Class Family Positions of the Seeds, Cube[1] & Cube[2]	Count of Beta Class Paths of Solutions Generated from the Seeds	#
1	111&112	2	111	112&111	6	1
2	111&121	2		121&111	6	2
3	111&211	2		211&111	6	3
4	114&113	2	114	113&114	6	4
5	114&124	2		124&114	6	5
6	114&214	2		214&114	6	6
7	141&142	2	141	142&141	6	7
8	141&131	2		131&141	6	8
9	141&241	2		241&141	6	9
10	144&143	2	144	143&144	6	10
11	144&134	2		134&144	6	11
12	144&244	2		244&144	6	12
13	411&412	2	411	412&411	6	13
14	411&421	2		421&411	6	14
15	411&311	2		311&411	6	15
16	414&413	2	414	413&414	6	16
17	414&424	2		424&414	6	17
18	414&314	2		314&414	6	18
19	441&442	2	441	442&441	6	19
20	441&431	2		431&441	6	20
21	441&341	2		341&441	6	21
22	444&443	2	444	443&444	6	22
23	444&434	2		434&444	6	23
24	444&344	2		344&444	6	24

Total ==> 48

Total ==> 144

The First Path of Solution in Each of the Six Beta Class Families.

Beta Class Family #1

Family[112&111 First]		
112&111 First	412&411	
121&111	421&411	
211&111	311&411	
113&114	413&414	
124&114	424&414	
214&114	314&414	
142&141	442&441	
131&141	431&441	
241&141	341&441	
143&144	443&444	
134&144	434&444	
244&144	344&444	

Beta Class Family #2

Family[112&111 Second]		
112&111 Second	412&411	
121&111	421&411	
211&111	311&411	
113&114	413&414	
124&114	424&414	
214&114	314&414	
142&141	442&441	
131&141	431&441	
241&141	341&441	
143&144	443&444	
134&144	434&444	
244&144	344&444	

Beta Class Family #3

Family[112&111 Third]		
112&111 Third	412&411	
121&111	421&411	
211&111	311&411	
113&114	413&414	
124&114	424&414	
214&114	314&414	
142&141	442&441	
131&141	431&441	
241&141	341&441	
143&144	443&444	
134&144	434&444	
244&144	344&444	

Beta Class Family #4

Family[112&111 Fourth]		
112&111 Fourth	412&411	
121&111	421&411	
211&111	311&411	
113&114	413&414	
124&114	424&414	
214&114	314&414	
142&141	442&441	
131&141	431&441	
241&141	341&441	
143&144	443&444	
134&144	434&444	
244&144	344&444	

Beta Class Family #5

Family[112&111 Fifth]		
112&111 Fifth	412&411	
121&111	421&411	
211&111	311&411	
113&114	413&414	
124&114	424&414	
214&114	314&414	
142&141	442&441	
131&141	431&441	
241&141	341&441	
143&144	443&444	
134&144	434&444	
244&144	344&444	

Beta Class Family #6

Family[112&111 Sixth]		
112&111 Sixth	412&411	
121&111	421&411	
211&111	311&411	
113&114	413&414	
124&114	424&414	
214&114	314&414	
142&141	442&441	
131&141	431&441	
241&141	341&441	
143&144	443&444	
134&144	434&444	
244&144	344&444	

Paths of Solution in the First Two Physical Solutions

Alpha Class			
Family[111&112 First]			
111&112 First	411&412 Second		
111&121 Second	411&421 First		
111&211 First	411&311 Second		
114&113 Second	414&413 First		
114&124 First	414&424 Second		
114&214 Second	414&314 First		
141&142 Second	441&442 First		
141&131 First	441&431 Second		
141&241 Second	441&341 First		
144&143 First	444&443 Second		
144&134 Second	444&434 First		
144&244 First	444&344 Second		

Beta Class			
Family[112&111 First]			
112&111 First	412&411 Fourth		
121&111 Fourth	421&411 Third		
211&111 Third	311&411 Sixth		
113&114 Fourth	413&414 First		
124&114 Third	424&414 Fourth		
214&114 Sixth	314&414 Third		
142&141 Fourth	442&441 First		
131&141 Third	431&441 Fourth		
241&141 Sixth	341&441 Third		
143&144 First	443&444 Fourth		
134&144 Fourth	434&444 Third		
244&144 Third	344&444 Sixth		

Twenty-Four Select Transpositions that Build the Family[112&111 First]

	Known Member			Path of Rotation			The Family	
	Cube 1	Cube 2	Sequence of Generation	Slabs to Rotate	Amount in Degrees	Direction	Member Identified by the Transposition	Count of Transpositions to the Member
1	214	114	Sixth	Aisle	90	counter	112&111 First	**9**
2	142	141	Fourth	Floor	90	clockwise	121&111 Fourth	3
3	214	114	Sixth	Floor	90	counter	211&111 Third	3
4	142	141	Fourth	Floor	180		113&114 Fourth	4
5	112	111	First	Floor	90	clockwise	124&114 Third	3
6	112	111	First	Aisle	90	clockwise	214&114 Sixth	3
7	112	111	First	Row	90	counter	142&141 Fourth	3
8	112	111	First	Floor	90	counter	131&141 Third	3
9	214	114	Sixth	Floor	180		241&141 Sixth	4
10	112	111	First	Floor	180		143&144 First	5
11	214	114	Sixth	Row	90	counter	134&144 Fourth	3
12	214	114	Sixth	Floor	90	clockwise	244&144 Third	3
13	112	111	First	Row	90	clockwise	412&411 Fourth	3
14	131	141	Third	Row	180		421&411 Third	4
15	112	111	First	Aisle	90	counter	311&411 Sixth	3
16	112	111	First	Aisle	180		413&414 First	5
17	214	114	Sixth	Row	90	clockwise	424&414 Fourth	3
18	124	144	Third	Row	90	clockwise	314&414 Third	3
19	112	111	First	Row	180		442&441 First	5
20	131	141	Third	Aisle	90	counter	431&441 Fourth	3
21	142	141	Fourth	Aisle	90	counter	341&441 Third	3
22	142	141	Fourth	Aisle	180		443&444 Fourth	4
23	131	141	Third	Aisle	180		434&444 Third	4
24	214	114	Sixth	Row	180		344&444 Sixth	4

Total Count of Transpositions ==> 90

Appendix 5   Page 5

Slabs[Floor] inverted

Cube Number	Cube Number
16	9
17	10
26	11
27	12
28	15
29	18
32	25
33	30
57	31
58	34
59	43
60	44
61	45
62	50
63	51
64	56

Slabs[Row]

Cube Number	Cube Number
2	1
3	6
4	7
5	10
8	11
9	27
28	38
29	39
30	40
31	41
32	42
33	43
34	44
35	62
36	63
37	64

Slabs[Aisle]

Cube Number	Cube Number
1	3
2	31
33	32
34	36
35	40
42	41
43	44
48	45
49	46
50	47
51	54
52	55
53	56
58	57
59	60
64	63

Slabs[Floor]

Cube Number	Cube Number
1	7
2	8
3	13
4	14
5	19
6	24
20	35
21	36
22	37
23	38
39	41
40	42
47	46
48	49
53	52
54	55

Solution[112&111 First]

Tint	Cube Number	Floor	Aisle	Row	Position	Type of Cube	Cube Number
		Position in the 4x4x4 Array					
Dark	1	1	1	2	112	Straight	1
light	2	1	1	1	111	Corner	2
Dark	3	1	2	1	121	Straight	3
Light	4	1	3	1	131	Straight	4
Dark	5	1	4	1	141	Corner	5
Light	6	1	4	2	142	Corner	6
Dark	7	2	4	2	242	Corner	7
Light	8	2	4	1	241	Corner	8
Dark	9	3	4	1	341	Corner	9
Light	10	3	4	2	342	Corner	10
Dark	11	3	3	2	332	Corner	11
Light	12	3	3	3	333	Corner	12
Dark	13	2	3	3	233	Corner	13
Light	14	2	3	4	234	Corner	14
Dark	15	3	3	4	334	Straight	15
Light	16	4	3	4	434	Corner	16
Dark	17	4	4	4	444	Corner	17
Light	18	3	4	4	344	Straight	18
Dark	19	2	4	4	244	Straight	19
Light	20	1	4	4	144	Corner	20
Dark	21	1	3	4	134	Corner	21
Light	22	1	3	3	133	Corner	22
Dark	23	1	4	3	143	Corner	23
Light	24	2	4	3	243	Corner	24
Dark	25	3	4	3	343	Straight	25
Light	26	4	4	3	443	Straight	26
Dark	27	4	4	2	442	Straight	27
Light	28	4	4	1	441	Corner	28
Dark	29	4	3	1	431	Corner	29
Light	30	3	3	1	331	Corner	30
Dark	31	3	2	1	321	Corner	31
Light	32	4	2	1	421	Corner	32

Pink

Left	Right
7	1
8	2
13	3
14	4
19	5
24	6
35	20
36	21
37	22
38	23
41	39
42	40
46	47
49	48
52	53
55	54

Yellow

Left	Right
12	14
13	15
22	16
23	17
24	18
25	19
26	20
45	21
46	51
47	52
48	53
49	54
50	55
59	56
60	57
61	58

Blue

Left	Right
4	5
11	6
12	7
13	8
14	9
15	10
16	17
21	18
22	19
29	20
30	23
37	24
38	25
39	26
61	27
62	28

White

Left	Right
9	16
10	17
11	26
12	27
15	28
18	29
25	32
30	33
31	57
34	58
43	59
44	60
45	61
50	62
51	63
56	64

Dark/Light	No.	d1	d2	d3	Code	Type	No.
Dark	33	4	1	1	411	Corner	33
Light	34	3	1	1	311	Straight	34
Dark	35	2	1	1	211	Corner	35
Light	36	2	2	1	221	Straight	36
Dark	37	2	3	1	231	Corner	37
Light	38	2	3	2	232	Corner	38
Dark	39	1	3	2	132	Corner	39
Light	40	1	2	2	122	Corner	40
Dark	41	2	2	2	222	Corner	41
Light	42	2	1	2	212	Corner	42
Dark	43	3	1	2	312	Corner	43
Light	44	3	2	2	322	Corner	44
Dark	45	3	2	3	323	Corner	45
Light	46	2	2	3	223	Straight	46
Dark	47	1	2	3	123	Corner	47
Light	48	1	1	3	113	Corner	48
Dark	49	2	1	3	213	Straight	49
Light	50	3	1	3	313	Corner	50
Dark	51	3	1	4	314	Corner	51
Light	52	2	1	4	214	Straight	52
Dark	53	1	1	4	114	Corner	53
Light	54	1	2	4	124	Corner	54
Dark	55	2	2	4	224	Straight	55
Light	56	3	2	4	324	Straight	56
Dark	57	4	2	4	424	Corner	57
Light	58	4	1	4	414	Corner	58
Dark	59	4	1	3	413	Corner	59
Light	60	4	2	3	423	Straight	60
Dark	61	4	3	3	433	Corner	61
Light	62	4	3	2	432	Corner	62
Dark	63	4	2	2	422	Straight	63
Light	64	4	1	2	412	Straight	64

Slabs[Aisle] out of the Six Digital Solutions from Seeds[214&114]

First	Second	Third	Fourth	Fifth	214&114 Sixth
Slabs of Aisle	Slabs of Aisle	Slabs of Aisle	Slabs of Aisle	Slabs of Aisle	Slabs of Aisle
1	1	1	1	1	1
2	2	2	2	2	2
3	3	3	16	16	33
4	4	4	17	17	34
5	5	5	26	26	35
6	6	6	27	27	42
9	12	20	28	28	43
10	13	21	33	33	48
14	14	22	34	34	49
15	15	23	35	35	50
16	16	39	36	36	51
17	17	40	37	37	52
18	18	47	38	38	53
19	19	48	39	39	58
20	20	53	40	40	59
21	21	54	41	41	64
7	7	7	3	3	3
8	8	8	10	10	31
11	9	13	11	11	32
12	10	14	12	12	36
13	11	19	15	15	40
22	22	24	18	18	41
23	23	35	25	25	44
24	24	36	29	29	45
25	25	37	30	30	46
26	26	38	31	31	47
35	35	41	32	32	54
36	36	42	42	42	55
37	37	46	43	43	56
62	62	49	44	44	57
63	63	52	61	61	60
64	64	55	62	62	63

Box	Left	Right
1 (shaded)	4, 11, 12, 13, 14, 15, 16, 21, 22, 29, 30, 37, 38, 39, 61, 62	5, 6, 7, 8, 9, 10, 17, 18, 19, 20, 23, 24, 25, 26, 27, 28
2	4, 8, 9, 13, 14, 19, 24, 45, 46, 47, 54, 55, 56, 57, 60, 63	5, 6, 7, 20, 21, 22, 23, 48, 49, 50, 51, 52, 53, 58, 59, 64
3	4, 8, 9, 13, 14, 19, 24, 45, 46, 47, 54, 55, 56, 57, 60, 63	5, 6, 7, 20, 21, 22, 23, 48, 49, 50, 51, 52, 53, 58, 59, 64
4	9, 10, 11, 12, 15, 18, 25, 30, 31, 34, 43, 44, 45, 50, 51, 56	16, 17, 26, 27, 28, 29, 32, 33, 57, 58, 59, 60, 61, 62, 63, 64
5	27, 30, 31, 34, 38, 39, 44, 45, 46, 47, 48, 49, 50, 59, 60, 61	28, 29, 32, 33, 40, 41, 42, 43, 51, 52, 53, 54, 55, 56, 57, 58
6	27, 30, 31, 34, 38, 39, 44, 45, 46, 47, 48, 49, 50, 59, 60, 61	28, 29, 32, 33, 40, 41, 42, 43, 51, 52, 53, 54, 55, 56, 57, 58

Slabs[Row] out of the Six Digital Solutions from Seeds[442&441]

Sol[442&441 First] Slabs of Row	Sol[442&441 Fourth] Slabs of Row	Second Slabs of Row	Fifth Slabs of Row	Third Slabs of Row	Sixth Slabs of Row
2	2	2	2	2	2
3	3	3	3	3	3
4	4	4	4	4	4
5	5	5	5	5	5
8	8	37	37	37	37
9	9	38	38	38	38
28	28	41	41	41	41
29	29	42	42	42	42
30	30	57	57	57	57
31	31	58	58	58	58
32	32	59	59	59	59
33	33	60	60	60	60
34	34	61	61	61	61
35	35	62	62	62	62
36	36	63	63	63	63
37	37	64	64	64	64
1	1	1	1	1	1
6	6	6	6	6	6
7	7	7	7	7	7
10	10	8	8	8	8
11	11	11	11	9	9
27	27	12	12	10	10
38	38	13	13	11	11
39	39	36	36	36	36
40	40	39	39	39	39
41	41	40	40	40	40
42	42	43	43	43	43
43	43	44	44	44	44
44	44	45	45	45	45
62	62	50	50	50	50
63	63	51	51	51	51
64	64	56	56	56	56

12	13	14	15	16	21	22	31	32	33	34	35	46	49	52	55	17	18	19	20	23	24	25	26	27	28	29	30	47	48	53	54
12	13	14	15	16	21	22	31	32	33	34	35	46	49	52	55	17	18	19	20	23	24	25	26	27	28	29	30	47	48	53	54

9	10	14	15	16	21	22	31	32	33	34	35	46	49	52	55	17	18	19	20	23	24	25	26	27	28	29	30	47	48	53	54
9	10	14	15	16	21	22	31	32	33	34	35	46	49	52	55	17	18	19	20	23	24	25	26	27	28	29	30	47	48	53	54

12	13	22	23	24	25	26	45	46	47	48	49	50	59	60	61	14	15	16	17	18	19	20	21	51	52	53	54	55	56	57	58
12	13	22	23	24	25	26	45	46	47	48	49	50	59	60	61	14	15	16	17	18	19	20	21	51	52	53	54	55	56	57	58

Slabs[Floor] out of the Six Digital Solutions from Seeds[442&441]

Sol[442&441 First] Slabs of Floor	Second Slabs of Floor	Third Slabs of Floor	Fourth Slabs of Floor	Fifth Slabs of Floor	Sixth Slabs of Floor
16	28	28	5	5	5
17	29	29	6	6	6
26	32	32	7	7	7
27	33	33	8	20	20
28	40	40	9	21	21
29	41	41	10	22	22
32	42	42	17	23	23
33	43	43	18	48	48
57	51	51	19	49	49
58	52	52	20	50	50
59	53	53	23	51	51
60	54	54	24	52	52
61	55	55	25	53	53
62	56	56	26	58	58
63	57	57	27	59	59
64	58	58	28	64	64
9	27	27	4	4	4
10	30	30	11	8	8
11	31	31	12	9	9
12	34	34	13	13	13
15	38	38	14	14	14
18	39	39	15	19	19
25	44	44	16	24	24
30	45	45	21	45	45
31	46	46	22	46	46
34	47	47	29	47	47
43	48	48	30	54	54
44	49	49	37	55	55
45	50	50	38	56	56
50	59	59	39	57	57
51	60	60	61	60	60
56	61	61	62	63	63

Box 1 (two rows):

3	10	11	12	15	18	25	29	30	31	32	42	43	44	61	62	1	2	16	17	26	27	28	33	34	35	36	37	38	39	40	41
3	10	11	12	15	18	25	29	30	31	32	42	43	44	61	62	1	2	16	17	26	27	28	33	34	35	36	37	38	39	40	41

Box 2:

3	31	32	36	40	41	44	45	46	47	54	55	56	57	60	63	1	2	33	34	35	42	43	48	49	50	51	52	53	58	59	64

Box 3 (two rows):

7	8	11	12	13	22	23	24	25	26	35	36	37	62	63	64	1	2	3	4	5	6	9	10	14	15	16	17	18	19	20	21
7	8	9	10	11	22	23	24	25	26	35	36	37	62	63	64	1	2	3	4	5	6	12	13	14	15	16	17	18	19	20	21

Box 4 (pink):

7	8	13	14	19	24	35	36	37	38	41	42	46	49	52	55	1	2	3	4	5	6	20	21	22	23	39	40	47	48	53	54

Appendix 6
All About Harry

See Section 3.5 "Let's Give a Look at Harry's Work"

About Developing Harry

Harry is a macro attached to a Microsoft Excel file. The name of the file is "Solve - S64 - One-at-a-Time - 20210810.xlsm". The macro is a VBA subroutine named "Solve_S64_All_2seed". "Harry" is the macro's nickname. Harry's template is a worksheet in the same Excel file. Harry's system specification is simple: Generate solutions to the King Snake Puzzle. This discourse is about Harry's operational design, his inputs, and his outputs. There are many references to Harry's Visual Basic source code listing, his template, and his output named "Solution 111 and 112 First".

Notice: Harry does no syntax check on the seeds to assure that the coordinates are, indeed, integer numbers ranging from one to four; nor to assure that the user has placed cube(1) and cube(2) in adjacent spaces of the 4x4x4 array. Also, he does not check the data in the column labelled "Type of Cube" to assure that the entries on the template have not been contaminated.

Comments: In the initial phase of my building and testing Harry, I had not included the output of the progress reports nor the counts of backups. Instead, I had Harry writing to the template every time he successfully placed a cube. Very early, after I had some confidence that Harry's logic was satisfactory, I started him going to generate a solution and then left him alone for a couple of hours. When I came back to check on him he was still running.

I remembered from the old days that too much I/O could contribute to that kind of problem. So along came Harry version 2, in which Harry outputs data regarding placement of cubes only when he has successfully placed cube(64). But he was still taking a long time. I got anxious. Along came Version 3, in which he outputs the progress reports to help sooth my impatient soul.

Next, I got curious about Harry's behavior. What is he doing in all that time? Hence version 4. He now writes the backup counts to the template. To me, they are very high numbers. Makes me wonder how any human, without descriptions of solutions as generated by Harry, is ever able to solve the puzzle. The count of backups required in the generation of "Solution 111 and 112" is 7, 926, 261! Leads me to wonder whether there is a flaw in Harry's logic.

Then came the requirement for Version 5, to generate more than one solution from a pair of seeds. One morning, in that time between being asleep and being awake, it came to me. Back out the successfully placed cube(64)!

Harry's inputs: Harry has three inputs. He reads all of them from his template. One of them needs no setting by the user. It is the configuration of the snake's cubes specified per cube number. See the column on the template labeled "Type of Cube". The second input is the user's specification of the seeds, namely the coordinates for cube(1) and cube(2). See the columns labeled "Floor", "Aisle", and "Row" on the template. The third input? Harry reads it from cell T08 of the template and it's another user input. Harry calls it "Desired Solution Name." It tells Harry which solution to output to the template. If it says "Third" Harry will generate three solutions and output only the third to the template. Harry can generate as many as six solutions per pair of seeds.

Harry's outputs: Harry has a couple of outputs to the template that are visible during his operation. They are output as progress reports to give the user an understanding that Harry is working away at finding a solution, that he is not in and endless loop. As he starts up, to let the user know that he is looking for the first solution, he will show "First" in cell T09. He updates the report as he goes along to let the user know which solution he is generating at the time. Harry outputs the second progress report when his touch count reaches 1,000,000. What is his touch count? It shows the count of times "n" has been incremented. And when the touch count reaches a million, he outputs the count of cubes that have been backed out of the 4x4x4 array of the solution. He outputs this number to cell T11.

Harry's Visual Basic code exists in eight sections:
(1) Define data structures and read in data from the template,
(2) Go process for completion, or output a progress report,
(3) Increment "n" and begin the calculation of coordinates for cube(n),
(4) Calculate coordinates for cube(n) when cube(n-1) is of type "Straight",
(5) Pick up coordinates for cube(n) when cube(n-1) is of type "Corner",
(6) Build the Neighbor array for cube(n) of type "Corner",
(7) Back out cube(n) and decrement "n",
(8) Output data describing the solution, or backout cube(64),

There are many comments included within the VBA code. They are presented in italics. The comments are intended to help with understanding the processes. The following descriptions are provided to help a bit more.

(1) **Define data structures and read in data from the template** -
In this section, in addition to reading in data from the template, Harry outputs the two progress reports to cells T09 and T11 for the first time. Because the **Neighbor** array for cube(2) has not yet been generated, he sets "n" equal 2 and transfers to section 6, location C600, to generate neighbors for cube(2).

(2) Location A500: **Go process for completion, or output the progress report**:
When cube(64) has been successfully placed, indicating that a solution is available for output to the template, Harry jumps to location Z600 to process for completion. Otherwise, he processes the output of the progress report, T11 on the template.

(3) Location A520: **Increment "n" and begin the calculation of coordinates for cube(n)**: Harry calculates the position for cube (n) depending on the type of cube(n-1). When cube(n-1) is "Straight" then the position for cube(n) is a function of the positions of both cube(n-1) and cube (n-2).

(4) Location A530: **Calculate coordinates for cube(n) when cube(n-1) is of type "Straight"** – Harry calls subroutine "Calculate Position" and "OneCoordinate" to do the work. He then compares the new position to positions already occupied in the 4x4x4 array. When he finds a duplicate, he transfers to location B500 to back out cube(n). Otherwise, he lets the new position stand. If the successfully placed cube(n) is of type "Corner" he transfers to location C600 to generate the Neighbor" array for cube(n).

(5) Location C500: **Pick up coordinates for cube(n) when cube(n-1) is of type "Corner"**: Harry examines the **Neighbor** array of cube(n-1) to find a position for cube(n). When he finds the Neighbor array to be empty, he transfers to location B500 to backout cube(n). Not empty? He lifts a position code from the Neighbor array of cube(n-1), calculates the coordinates for cube(n) from the position code, and places cube(n) in the 4x4x4 array of the solution. When cube(n) is of type Straight, the work is done for cube(n) and Harry transfers to location A500. For cube(n) of type Corner, Harry transfers to C600 to build the Neighbor array for cube(n).

(6) Location C600: **Build the Neighbor array for cube(n) of type "Corner"**: When I work at putting the snake back in its cage, I take each step a bit differently from Harry. Harry processes one cube at a time. I process a segment at a time. I look at a segment of consecutive cubes that begin with cube(n) and then at the space available around cube(n-1), the last cube I placed successfully. When I see available space, I'll push and twist the cubes of the snake that are trailing off away from me until I get them lined up to place them. And then I might see that I must also twist cube(n-1). It's a corner cube and it is not aimed at the space available for cube(n).

Harry accomplishes this process by maintaining and using the arrays **Neighbor** and **Available**. Harry populates these two arrays during the process of placing a corner cube. Something to look for: If Harry can't find any available neighbors for cube(n) he branches to location B500 to back out the Corner cube(n). The VBA code for this process begins at location C600 and ends with a branch to A500, just before location B500. It's a lengthy process.

(7) Location B500: **Back out cube(n) and decrement "n"**: The backout process is my favorite. It is so clean. First. Harry cleans out the arrays where data is stored describing cube(n). Then he **decrements "n".** At this point what used to be cube(n) no longer has a place in the 4x4x4 array. Harry examines data for the new cube(n) looking for a Corner cube with at least one neighbor available. If the new cube(n) is not the cube he's looking for then he goes to location B550 and backs out another cube(n)!

When Harry backs into a Corner cube with at least one neighbor available his search is over. At location B600 he tallies another "backup returned" and transfers to location A500 where the process starts going forward again with **incrementing "n".**

(8) Location Z500: **Output data describing the desired solution, or backout cube(64)**: This process begins when cube(64) has been successfully placed in the 4x4x4 array. The success in placing cube(64) is the signal that a solution has been generated. If it is the desired solution, then it's time to copy its data to the template. Harry's work is done. But if it is not the desired solution then Harry must start looking for yet another solution. How does he do that? By backing out cube(64)!

```vba
Option Explicit
Sub Solve_S64_All_2seed()
' Version 2, from file "Solve S64 One-at-a-time - 20210810.xlsm"
' August 13, 2021
'This macro generates as many as six solutions from one pair of seeds.


Range("E6", "V71").Select 'The only other Range statement in this
                          'procedure is at Z900, just before the Exit sub.


Const SnakeLength As Integer = 64  'For the 4x4x4 array the value is 64.


Dim n As Integer 'Used as the index into the arrays with length = SnakeLength.
    ' n  is reserved for use as the index that controls the major loop
    ' in this process.
Dim i As Integer
Dim k As Integer
Dim p As Integer
Dim w As Integer
Dim x As Integer


Dim Floor(1 To SnakeLength) As Integer  'the first of the three coordinates
    'of the position of a cube in the array that is the solution.
    'Values are 1, 2, 3, and 4; ranging from bottom floor to top floor.


Dim Aisle(1 To SnakeLength) As Integer  'the second of the three coordinates of
    'position. Values are 1, 2, 3, and 4; ranging from left aisle to right aisle.


Dim Row(1 To SnakeLength) As Integer   'the third of the three coordinates of
    'position. Values are 1, 2,3, and 4; ranging from front row to back row.


Dim PositionCode(1 To SnakeLength) As Integer
    'three digits representing the coordinates of the position.
    'A code of 312 is a code for Floor = 3, Aisle = 1, and Row = 2.


Dim CubeType(1 To SnakeLength) As String
    'CubeType has one of two values: "Corner" or "Straight".
    'Populated from the template worksheet.
```

>>>

'===

'*All about the "Neighbor" arrays.*

Dim Neighbor(1 To SnakeLength, 1 To 4) As Integer

'This array contains position codes, as many as 4 codes per corner cube.
'to define the neighboring positions for a cube to follow the
'corner cube in the 4x4x4 array. The first index is "n" for cube(n)
'and this array has no meaning when n points to a '"straight" cube.

Dim Available(1 To SnakeLength) As Integer *'Indexed by "n".*

' "Available" is the count of neighboring spaces
' still available for the cube at "n + 1".
' 0 indicates that no more are available.

Dim OnePosition(1 To 3) As Integer

' Contains coordinates for ONE POSITION in the 4x4x4 arrqy.
' Index 1 contains a coordinate for floor.
' Index 2 contains a coordinate for aisle.
' Index 3 contains a coordinate for row.

Dim OnePosCode As Integer

Dim FAR(1 To 6, 1 To 3) As Integer

'FAR stands for Floor, Aisle, Row
'The FAR array is used in calculating the position codes to be stored
'in the Neighbor array of a "Corner" cube. In the FAR array
'the index 6 is the number of neighbors of a cube, a neighbor
'for each face of the cube. The index 3 is for the coordinates
'of the neighbor: Index 1 is Floor, Index 2 is Aisle, Index 3 is Row

Dim FARcode(1 To 6) As Integer *'FARcodes are position codes.*

'The FARcodes are calculated from the coordinates in the FAR array.

Dim Include(1 To 6) As String *'An indicator "Yes" or "No" whether to*

'include the FARcode in the Neighbor array.

'=============================
'=============================

'About Backups.

Dim BackupsBegun(1 To SnakeLength) As Long
Dim BackupsReturned(1 To SnakeLength) As Long

'When n points to a corner cube then BackupsReturned shows
'the number of times a backup procedure has successfully
'CONCLUDED with n pointing to that cube.

Dim TotalBackups As Long
    TotalBackups = 0

' This count is displayed but not printed in the report.
' It is used as a progress repor. The witness can see this number
' on the display. It gives assurance that the program is working
' as planned.

Dim TouchCount As Long

'The count of entries to A500, the top of the big loop on n.

    TouchCount = 0

' TotalBackups is displayed each time
' the TouchCount reaches 1,000,000.

Dim Trouble As String
Dim Temp As Integer

    'Housekeep some columns
For w = 1 To SnakeLength
    BackupsBegun(w) = 0
    ActiveCell(w, 11) = ""
    BackupsReturned(w) = 0
    ActiveCell(w, 12) = "" *'Count of backups successfully completed*
Next [w]

'=================================
    'Initialize the array CubeType from column I on the worksheet.
For w = 1 To SnakeLength
  CubeType(w) = ActiveCell(w, 5)
Next [w]

'Read in the settings for the two seeds, w=1 and w=2
'from the worksheet.
For w = 1 To 2
    Floor(w) = ActiveCell(w, 1) *'Column E*

>>>

```
        Aisle(w) = ActiveCell(w, 2)  'Column F
        Row(w) = ActiveCell(w, 3)  'Column G
Next [w]


    'Initialize the setttings of PositionCode for the seeds.
For w = 1 To 2
        PositionCode(w) = (100 * Floor(w)) + (10 * Aisle(w)) + Row(w)
        ActiveCell(w, 4) = PositionCode(w) ' Index 4 is Column H
Next [w]


        'Set the BackupLimit to point to the first corner
        'cube in the snake.
Dim BackupLimit As Integer
BackupLimit = 0
For w = 1 To SnakeLength
        If (CubeType(w) = "Corner") Then BackupLimit = w
            'When BackupLimit is > 0 then
            'the second corner cube has been found
        If (BackupLimit > 0) Then Exit For
            ' Don't have to continue through the whole of the snake
            ' after the BackupLimit has been found.
Next [w]


Dim DesiredSolutionName As String
Dim DesiredSolutionNumber As Integer
Dim CurrentSolutionNumber As Integer
Dim CurrentSolutionName As String
Dim SolutionName(1 To 6) As String
        SolutionName(1) = "First"
        SolutionName(2) = "Second"
        SolutionName(3) = "Third"
        SolutionName(4) = "Fourth"
        SolutionName(5) = "Fifth"
        SolutionName(6) = "Sixth"

        DesiredSolutionName = ActiveCell(3, 16) 'Cell T08 on the template
        DesiredSolutionNumber = 0
```

```
       For w = 1 To 6
           If (DesiredSolutionName = SolutionName(w)) Then _
               DesiredSolutionNumber = w
        Next [w]
       If (DesiredSolutionNumber = 0) Then GoTo Z900 'Trouble
       CurrentSolutionNumber = 1
       CurrentSolutionName = "First"
       ActiveCell(4, 16) = CurrentSolutionName ' Cell T09 On the template
```

n = 2 *' Begin the loop on n with n = 2, pointing to the last cube*
'that was successfully placed,
'============================
'This is the end of the housekeeping.
''Begin the loop on n with n = 2, pointing to the last cube
'that was successfully placed. At the beginning,
'when CubeType(2) = "Corner"
'start the processing at C600 in order to build
'the Neighbor array for the seed at n=2.

A400: If (CubeType(2) = "Corner") Then GoTo C600
*'*************** HERE WE GO!!* ***************
'***
'***

'This is the TOP OF THE BIG LOOP ON "n" to place cube
'coordinates in the arrays Floor, Aisle, and Row,
'to solve the 4x4x4 Snake Puzzle.

A500: *' There are four branches to A500.*
' 1:: After positioning cube(n) when cube(n) is "Straight"
'   and cube(n-1) is "Straight".
' 2:: After positioning cube(n) when cube(n) is "Straight"
'   and cube(n-1) is "Corner).
' 3:: When cube(n) is "Corner", after building the cube's neighbor array.
' 4:: At the successful conclusion of executing a backup process.
''==================================

       If ((n = BackupLimit) And (Available(n) = 0)) Then GoTo B700
               'The game is over. No solution this time.
       If (n = SnakeLength) Then GoTo Z500
               ' Ring bells, Blow bugles, A solution has been found.
               ' Go see whether it is the desired solution.

>>>

' Here: n is less than SnakeLength.

TouchCount = TouchCount + 1

> *' Display the updated TotalBackups*
> *' when TouchCount reaches 1,000,000.*

If (TouchCount = 1000000) Then

> **ActiveCell(6, 16) = TotalBackups** *' Cell T11 on the template*
> **TouchCount = 0**

End If

'++

> *'Here: there are more cubes to be positioned in the 4x4x4 array.*
>> '*************************************
>>
>> '*************************************

A520: n = n + 1 *'See what can be done for the next cube.*

> '*********** *This is the only instruction in the whole*
> '*********** *routine where "n" is incremented.*

' The first big branch in the flow:
' Processing begins with establishing a position for cube(n)
' depending on the type of CUBE(n-1)!! That's "N MINUS ONE".

> **If (CubeType(n - 1) = "Straight") Then GoTo A530**
>> *' Calculate coordinates for cube(n) from*
>> *' the coordinates of cube(n-1) and cube(n-2).*

A525: If (CubeType(n - 1) = "Corner") Then GoTo C500

> *' Pick up a position for cube(n) from*
> *' the Neighbor array of cube(n-1).*

A530: *' Here: CubeType(n-1) is "Straight".*

> *' Calculate coordinates for cube(n) from*
> *' the coordinates of cube(n-1) and cube(n-2).*

Trouble = "AOK"

Call CalculatePosition(n, Floor(), Aisle(), Row(), Trouble)

> *'Trouble indicates invalid coordinate of zero or five*
> *'meaning there is no space available to folllow*
> *'the CubeType of Straight at n-1.*

If (Trouble = "Yes") Then GoTo B500 *'Back out cube(n).*

PositionCode(n) = (Floor(n) * 100) + (Aisle(n) * 10) + Row(n)

>>>

'===================================
            'Here: Floor(n), Aisle(n), and Row(n) are valid.
            'If the position is already occupied then back out cube(n).

For i = 1 To (n - 1)
    If (PositionCode(i) = PositionCode(n)) Then GoTo B500
Next [i]
'***

'Here: Cube(n) is successfully positioned.
' This is the end of the processing to establish position for cube(n)
    ' when cube(n-1) is straight. What now for cube(n)?

If (CubeType(n) = "Straight") Then
    GoTo A500 *'to begin processing for the next cube.*
ElseIf (CubeType(n) = "Corner") Then
    GoTo C600 *'to build the Neighbor array for cube(n).*
End If
'**

C500: *'C500 is entered from A525.*
    'Here: CubeType(n-1) = "Corner"
    '   CubeType   (n-1) =   "Corner"
    ' CubeType   (n-1) =   "Corner"
    '

    'Cube(n) is either Straight or Corner.
    'Cube(n) is either Straight or Corner.
    'Cube(n) is either Straight or Corner.

    ' Here: Pick up a position for cube(n)
    ' when cube(n-1) is "Corner"
If (Available(n - 1) = 0) Then GoTo B500
    'The Neighbor array at n-1 is empty.
    'Go to backup. No space is known for Cube(n).

    'Here: There is at least one neighbor's space still available.
PositionCode(n) = Neighbor(n - 1, Available(n - 1))
    'The Position is now taken. It is no longer available.
    'Remove it from the array of Neighbors.
Neighbor(n - 1, Available(n - 1)) = 0
    ' Decrement the count of availabe neghbors.
Available(n - 1) = Available(n - 1) - 1

'Now: Translate the PositionCode into coordinates.
```
Floor(n) = Int(PositionCode(n) / 100)
    Temp = PositionCode(n) - (Floor(n) * 100)
Aisle(n) = Int(Temp / 10)
Row(n) = PositionCode(n) - (Floor(n) * 100) - (Aisle(n) * 10)
```
' Here: Coordinates have been set for cube(n),
' be it either a corner cube or a straight cube.

' This is the end of processing to establish position
' for cube(n) when CubeType(n-1) is "Corner".
' What now for cube(n)?
```
If (CubeType(n) = "Corner") Then
    GoTo C600 ' to build the neighbor array
ElseIf (CubeType(n) = "Straight") Then
    GoTo A500 ' begin processing for the next cube
End If
```
'==

C600: 'Here: Cube(n) is of type "Corner" and its position is set.
'It's time to calculate the candidate positions for Cube(n+1),
'the neighbors of Cube(n). In other words,
'populate the Neighbor array. It's a sneaky job, a lengthy process.
```
For k = 1 To 6
```
'Cube(n) has 6 faces and there is <u>possibility</u> of position
'for a neighbor at each face. Each of the 6 positions has
'3 coordinates. 3 times 6 is 18 coordinates.
'Set all 18 coordinates in the FAR array.
```
    FAR(k, 1) = Floor(n)
    FAR(k, 2) = Aisle(n)
    FAR(k, 3) = Row(n)
Next [k]
```
'Modify 6 of the 18 coordinates in the FAR array to identify 6 positions.
```
FAR(1, 3) = Row(n) − 1 'One row behind cube(n)
FAR(2, 3) = Row(n) + 1 'One row in front of cube(n)
FAR(3, 2) = Aisle(n) − 1 'One aisle to the left of cube(n)
FAR(4, 2) = Aisle(n) + 1 'One aisle to the right of cube(n)
FAR(5, 1) = Floor(n) - 1 'One floor below cube(n)
FAR(6, 1) = Floor(n) + 1 'One floor above cube(n)
```
'Here: The array FAR contains positions for
'ALL six of the possible neighbors of Cube(n).

>>>

'The following steps identify the positions that are
' not to be INCLUDED in the Neighbor array.
'There are three types.
'1-- The positions with coordinates outside the 4x4x4 array.
'2-- The positions in the 4x4x4 array that are already occupied,
'3-- The position that is the "straight ahead" position
'   when cube(n-1) is of type "Straight".

For k = 1 To 6
    'Housekeep array "Include"
  Include(k) = "Yes"
Next [k]

For k = 1 To 6
  For p = 1 To 3 *' 18 coordinates, one coordinate at a time.*
    If ((FAR(k, p) < 1) Or (FAR(k, p) > 4)) Then Include(k) = "No"
  Next [p] *' For p = 1 To 3*

  If (Include(k) = "Yes") Then
    FARcode(k) = (100 * FAR(k, 1)) + (10 * FAR(k, 2)) + FAR(k, 3)
  Else: FARcode(k) = 0
  End If
Next [k] *' For k = 1 To 6*
  'Here: The Include array indicates "Do not include" for the positions
  'with invalid coordinates, and the FARcode array is built.

' Determine whether the FARcodes currently marked for inclusion identify
' positions in the 4x4x4 array that already have cubes assignd to them,
' and if so, mark the Include array for those FARcodes "No, do not include".

For k = 1 To 6

    If (Include(k) = "Yes") Then

        ' Compare FARcodes to PositionCodes.
        ' Start the loop with cube(n-1) and work backwards.
        ' Save some processing time.

        p = n - 1

        Do Until (p = 0)

            If (PositionCode(p) = FARcode(k)) Then

                Include(k) = "No"

                Exit Do

            End If *' If (PositionCode(p)*

        p = p - 1

        Loop *'Do Until*

    End If *' If (Include(k) = "Yes")*

Next [k] *' For k = 1 to 6*

'One more exclusion to consider. It is the position that would
' be the "straight ahead" position if cube(n) were a cube type of
' "Straight". Generate OnePosCode to compare to the entries
' in the array FARcode.

  ' Trouble calculating OnePosition indicates that
  ' OnePosCode is already marked for exclusion
  ' due to having a coordinate out of range.

Trouble = "AOK"

Call OneCoordinate(Floor(n - 1), Floor(n), OnePosition(1), Trouble)

Call OneCoordinate(Aisle(n - 1), Aisle(n), OnePosition(2), Trouble)

Call OneCoordinate(Row(n - 1), Row(n), OnePosition(3), Trouble)

If (Trouble = "Yes") Then GoTo C615

    'Here: The array OnePosition now contains the coordinates
    ' of the space that is in line with cube(n-1) and cube(n). The Neighbor
    ' array allows ONLY spaces that are at right angle to that line.
    ' This position, then, cannot be included in
    ' the Neighbor array for cube(n).

OnePosCode = (100 * OnePosition(1)) + (10 * OnePosition(2)) + OnePosition(3)

>>

```
          For k = 1 To 6
              If (OnePosCode = FARcode(k)) Then
                    Include(k) = "No"
                    Exit For
              End If
          Next [k] 'For k = 1 To 6
```

'================================

'Here: At last, The Include array is complete.
'Move data into the Neighbor array.

C615: 'First, Clean up some things.

```
          Available(n) = 0
          For p = 1 To 4
              Neighbor(n, p) = 0
          Next [p]
```

' Here: Move PosCodes from the FARcode array
            'into the Neighbor array.

```
          p = 6
          Do While (p > 0)
              If (Include(p) = "Yes") Then
```

' Here: Include FARcode(p) in the Neighbor array.

```
                    Available(n) = Available(n) + 1
                    Neighbor(n, Available(n)) = FARcode(p)
              End If
          p = p - 1
          Loop ' Do While
```

' What happens here if Available(n) = 0
' after the move to the Neighbor array????
' Back out Cube(n).That's what happens.

```
          If (Available(n) = 0) Then GoTo B500
```

' Notice: On the resulting Excel worksheet, no backups
' will begin on a "Straight" cube that follows a "Corner" cube.

' This is the end of the process that began at C600.

```
          GoTo A500      ' Begin processing for the next cube.
```

'==================================

B500: *'Begin Backup here -- knowing that cube(n) has trouble.*
        'Remember: When n=BackupLimit then CubeType(n) = Corner.

    BackupsBegun(n) = BackupsBegun(n) + 1

B550: **If (n = BackupLimit) And (Available(n) = 0) Then GoTo B700**
      ' All of the backups have already occurred. Game over.
    If (n < BackupLimit) Then GoTo B700
      ' How did we backup beyond the backup limit?

    'Here: Execute the backup .
    'Clean up for the rejected cube.
    Floor(n) = 0
    Aisle(n) = 0
    Row(n) = 0
    PositionCode(n) = 0
    For i = 1 To 4
       Neighbor(n, i) = 0
    Next [i]
    Available(n) = 0

    n = n - 1 *'This is the ONLY place in the whole process*
         'where n is decremented.
      ' With "n" decremented, one cube is "backed out".

      ' Now, Back up to the corner cube that can be used
      ' to restart the forward loop on n.
    If ((n = BackupLimit) And (Available(n) = 0)) Then GoTo B700
      ' Can't backup onto the cube at BackupLimit when it has no neighbors.
    If ((CubeType(n) = "Corner") And (Available(n) > 0)) Then _
      GoTo B600 *' This is it!!*
    GoTo B550 *' Go back out another cube.*

    'Here: n points to the corner cube needed
    ' to start going forward again in the loop on n.
B600: **BackupsReturned(n) = BackupsReturned(n) + 1**
    TotalBackups = TotalBackups + 1
    GoTo A500 *' The backup is successful, Jump to*
      ' the top of the forward loop on n, the BIG LOOP on n.

>>>

```
B700:   ActiveCell(6, 2) = "No solution was found."
            'There is no solution for seeds at n=1 and  n=2.
            'The game is over.
        GoTo Z900


Z500:   ' Here: A solution has been found. Upon entry here n = 64.
        If (CurrentSolutionNumber <> DesiredSolutionNumber) Then GoTo Z600
            'Go find the desired solution.


         ' Here: the desired solution has been found.
         ' Transfer the data to the Excel worksheet.
        For x = 1 To SnakeLength
            ActiveCell(x, 1) = Floor(x)                  ' Column E
            ActiveCell(x, 2) = Aisle(x)                  ' Column F
            ActiveCell(x, 3) = Row(x)                    ' Column G
            ActiveCell(x, 4) = PositionCode(x)           ' Column H


            If (BackupsBegun(x) <> 0) Then _
                ActiveCell(x, 11) = BackupsBegun(x)      ' Column O
            If (BackupsReturned(x) <> 0) Then _
                ActiveCell(x, 12) = BackupsReturned(x)  ' Column P


            If (CubeType(x) = "Corner") Then
                 ' Notice: This means that the Excel worksheet
                 ' shows only the final state of the Neighbor arrays.
                ActiveCell(x, 6) = Available(x)    'Column J
                For k = 1 To 4
                    If (Neighbor(x, k) <> 0) Then _
                        ActiveCell(x, k + 6) = Neighbor(x, k)
                            ' Cols K, L, M, and N
                Next [k]
            End If  '  If (CubeType(x) = "Corner")
        Next [x]  ' For x = 1 To SnakeLength
        GoTo Z900 ' The work is done.
        '=====================================
```

```
'======================================
Z600:  'Here: Look for another solution. Upon entry here, n = 64.
       CurrentSolutionNumber = CurrentSolutionNumber + 1
       For x = 1 To 6
           If (x = CurrentSolutionNumber) Then
                   CurrentSolutionName = SolutionName(x)
                   ActiveCell(4, 16) = CurrentSolutionName
           End If
       Next [x]
       GoTo B500 'Back out cube(64). Begin the search for another solution.


Z900:    n = n
               'Range("A1", "A1").Select
               'Close down the selection before doing something regrettable.
                   'SendKeys "{ESC}", True ' "True" means to wait for the action to occur.
         'Exit Sub
End Sub ' Solve_S64_All_2seed()
'======================================
Private Sub CalculatePosition(n As Integer, _
                       Floor() As Integer, _
                       Aisle() As Integer, _
                       Row() As Integer, _
                       Trouble As String)
       'Trouble is initialized by the calling routine.
       Call OneCoordinate(Floor(n - 2), Floor(n - 1), Floor(n), Trouble)
       Call OneCoordinate(Aisle(n - 2), Aisle(n - 1), Aisle(n), Trouble)
       Call OneCoordinate(Row(n - 2), Row(n - 1), Row(n), Trouble)
        'Trouble is set to "Yes" by "OneCoordinate" to indicate that
        'a coordinate is > 4 or < 1.
       Exit Sub
End Sub 'CalculatePosition
'======================================
```

```
'=======================================
Private Sub OneCoordinate(x1 As Integer, x2 As Integer, x3 As Integer, _
       Trouble As String)
' Trouble is initialized by the calling routine.
' The inputs to this subroutine are x1, x2, and Trouble.
' The outputs are x3 and Trouble
      x3 = x2
      If (x1 < x2) Then x3 = x2 + 1
      If (x1 > x2) Then x3 = x2 - 1
       If ((x3 > 4) Or (x3 < 1)) Then Trouble = "Yes"
      Exit Sub
End Sub 'OneCoordinate
'=======================================
```

August 15, 2021

#	Tint	Cube's Sequence Number i.e. ==> n	Floor	Aisle	Row	Position Code	Type of Cube	Count of Available Neighbors	AN 1	AN 2	AN 3	AN 4	Count of Backups Begun at n	Count of Backups Returned to n	Cube's Sequence Number i.e. ==> n	#
6	Dark	1	2	1	1	211	Straight								1	6
7	Light	2	1	1	1	111	Corner								2	7
8	Dark	3					Straight								3	8
9	Light	4					Straight								4	9
10	Dark	5					Corner								5	10
11	Light	6					Corner								6	11
12	Dark	7					Corner								7	12
13	Light	8					Corner								8	13
14	Dark	9					Corner								9	14
15	Light	10					Corner								10	15
16	Dark	11					Corner								11	16
17	Light	12					Corner								12	17
18	Dark	13					Corner								13	18
19	Light	14					Corner								14	19
20	Dark	15					Straight								15	20
21	Light	16					Corner								16	21
22	Dark	17					Corner								17	22
23	Light	18					Straight								18	23
24	Dark	19					Straight								19	24
25	Light	20					Corner								20	25
26	Dark	21					Corner								21	26
27	Light	22					Corner								22	27
28	Dark	23					Corner								23	28
29	Light	24					Straight								24	29
30	Dark	25					Straight								25	30
31	Light	26					Corner								26	31
32	Dark	27					Straight								27	32
33	Light	28					Corner								28	33
34	Dark	29					Corner								29	34
35	Light	30					Corner								30	35
36	Dark	31					Corner								31	36
37	Light	32					Corner								32	37

Desired First
Current

#	C	D	E	F	G	H	I	J	K	L	M	N	O	P	Q	R	S	T
38	Dark	33					Corner								33	38		
39	Light	34					Straight								34	39		
40	Dark	35					Corner								35	40		
41	Light	36					Straight								36	41		
42	Dark	37					Corner								37	42		
43	Light	38					Corner								38	43		
44	Dark	39					Corner								39	44		
45	Light	40					Corner								40	45		
46	Dark	41					Corner								41	46		
47	Light	42					Corner								42	47		
48	Dark	43					Corner								43	48		
49	Light	44					Corner								44	49		
50	Dark	45					Corner								45	50		
51	Light	46					Straight								46	51		
52	Dark	47					Corner								47	52		
53	Light	48					Corner								48	53		
54	Dark	49					Straight								49	54		
55	Light	50					Corner								50	55		
56	Dark	51					Corner								51	56		
57	Light	52					Straight								52	57		
58	Dark	53					Corner								53	58		
59	Light	54					Corner								54	59		
60	Dark	55					Straight								55	60		
61	Light	56					Straight								56	61		
62	Dark	57					Corner								57	62		
63	Light	58					Corner								58	63		
64	Dark	59					Corner								59	64		
65	Light	60					Straight								60	65		
66	Dark	61					Corner								61	66		
67	Light	62					Corner								62	67		
68	Dark	63					Straight								63	68		
69	Light	64					Straight								64	69		
	C	D	E	F	G	H	I	J	K	L	M	N	O	P	Q	R	S	T
			1	2	3	4	5	6	7	8	9	10	11	0		14	15	16
														12	13			

Backups Begun ==> (N, 10)

Backups Completed — <== Backups Completed (Q, 13)

Appendix 6 Page 23

Appendix 7

The Glossary

The Glossary

- Alpha Class and Beta Class – Each of Harry's 192 digital solutions is either an Alpha-Class solution or a Beta-class solution. An Alpha-Class solution places cube[1] in an ultimate corner. A Beta-Class solution places cube[2] in an ultimate corner. There are 48 Alpha-Class solutions: 8 ultimate corners, times 3 pairs of seeds per ultimate corner, times 2 sequences-of-generation per pair of seeds. The Beta-Class solutions have 6 sequences-of-generation per pair of seeds. That's 144 digital solutions in Beta Class.

- Adjacent positions or neighboring positions – Two positions in the 4x4x4 array are adjacent positions when the coordinates of their positions differ by a value of one, in one and only one coordinate. Examples: Pos[334] is above pos[234]. Pos]334] is to the left of pos[344]. Pos[112] is behind pos[111].

- Cage – The King Snake's cage is the 4x4x4 array of sixty-four cubic spaces. When I solve the puzzle, "I put the snake back in its cage."

- CC – An acronym used to refer to the small business named "Creative Crafthouse".

- Coordinates of the 4x4x4 array – Each of the sixty-four cubic spaces in the 4x4x4 array has three coordinates to name its position in the array. The coordinates are "Floor", "Aisle", and "Row". "Floor" ranges in value from bottom to top, "Aisle" ranges in value from left to right, and "Row" ranges in value from front to back. The names of the values are 1, 2, 3, and 4. The position named by the coordinates (1,1,1) is bottom floor, leftmost aisle, front row. See "Position".

- Corner cube - A cube in the snake in which the elastic string exits the cube through a face that is at right angle to the face of its entry. The elastic string turns a corner inside the cube. This causes the snake to turn a corner in its path through the 4x4x4 array of solution. Sometimes, in referring to a corner cube, only the word "corner" is used. See "Straight cube". See "Ultimate corner".

- Cube[n] – Read this as "cube sub n" or "cube n". When Harry has set the variable "n" to 23 then cube[n] refers to the 23rd cube in the snake. The 22nd cube, in this case, is cube[n-1], read as "cube sub n minus 1". There are also references to cube[n-2] and cube[n+1].

The Glossary

- Digital solution – One of Harry's 192 lists that identifies coordinates in a 4x4x4 array for each of the sixty-four cubes of the King Snake Puzzle. These lists specify 192 unique digital solutions. The two charts from Creative Crafthouse also identify digital solutions. They are two of Harry's 192 digital solutions.

- Eloise – The name used in referring to the Visual Basic macro that generates a digital solution for the small Snake Puzzle of twenty-seven cubes.

- External slab – The snake's cage has six external slabs. They are the six faces of the 4x4x4 array. The top floor of the array is one of these external slabs. It consists of the sixteen positions with the coordinate "Floor" having the value 4. The top floor of the array is slab[Floor 4]. See "Slab".

- Family of Solutions – There are twenty-four member solutions in a family of solutions. The first member is the mother solution. The mother solution originates in octant[111]. The name of the family is the name of the mother solution. The other twenty-three member solutions are siblings. Each member of the family is the object of transposition from a known member such as the mother. The family includes three members originating in each of the eight octants.

- FAR – An acronym for "Floor, Aisle, Row". "FAR" substitutes for the word "position" and for the word "coordinates".

- Frustrated transposition – An objective of transposing a digital solution is to identify the ordinal number of the sequence-of-generation for the solution being transposed to. The following is an error message used to reveal that transposing by rotating sol[112&111 First] on the path "slabs[Row] 90 degrees clockwise" is frustrated: "Transposition[197] is frustrated due to duplicate slabs[Row] in Sol[412&411 First] and Sol[412&411 Fourth]". Is the desired ordinal number "First" or "Fourth"? See "Resolve a frustrated transposition". Resolving the frustrated transposition[197] identifies sol[412&411 Fourth] to be a solution that is rotationally equivalent to sol[112&111 First].

The Glossary

- Gizmo – A name for the King Snake Puzzle in a solved state. A nickname for "physical solution".

- Harry – The name used in referring to the Visual Basic macro that generates digital solutions to the King Snake Puzzle.

- Inverted Slabs – A list of Slabs[Aisle], for instance, in which the cubes in Slab[Aisle 4] appear at the top of the list and cubes in slab[Aisle 1] appear at the bottom of the list.

- Margo – The name used in referring to the Visual Basic macro that counts digital solutions to the King Snake Puzzle.

- Names of the solutions - The names of the digital solutions are derived from inputs to Harry. If cube[1] of a solution sits at position[111], cube[2] sits at position[112], and the solution is the first one that Harry generates with cube[1] and cube[2] in these positions then the name of the solution is sol[111&112 First].

- Neighbor - Each of the cubic spaces in the 4x4x4 array of the King Snake Puzzle has three coordinates. They are Floor, Aisle, and Row. Two spaces are neighbors in the 4x4x4 array when one and only one of their coordinates differs in value and the difference is a value of one.

- Octant – An octant is a 2x2x2 array within the 4x4x4 array of the cage that holds the snake in solution. The 4x4x4 array is made up of eight octants, one at each of the eight ultimate corners. One of the positions in each octant is an ultimate corner. Each octant is named for its ultimate corner, e.g., octant[114]. See "Ultimate corner".

- Octant of origin – Each solution has an octant of origin. It is the octant that contains cube[1] and cube[2] of the solution. For an Alpha-Class solution the name of its octant of origin is the position of cube[1]. For a Beta-Class solution the name of its octant of origin is the position of cube[2]. Examples: The octant of origin for solution[114&113 First] is octant[114]. The octant of origin for solution[113&114 First] is also octant[114].

The Glossary

- Ordinal number or ordinal – Each solution is identified by the positions of its seeds and its sequence-of-generation with sequence-of-generation represented by an ordinal number, i.e. First, Second, Third, Fourth, Fifth, or Sixth.

- Path– The path of the snake through the 4x4x4 array of solution. Each of Harry's digital solutions describes one path, or one path of solution, or one solution.

- Physical solution– The 64 **wooden** cubes of the snake puzzle sitting in a 4x4x4 array, sometimes called "gizmo". There are **eight unique physical solutions** of the King Snake Puzzle, two in Alpha Class and six in Beta Class. A physical solution is named for the family of solutions that cohabits its cage. See "Cage". See "Alpha Class". See "Family of Solutions".

- Position or poscode or pos – the name of a position, minus the commas. Position "4,1,3" is position[413], poscode[413], or pos[413]. The numbers are the coordinates of the position: Floor, Aisle, and Row. Read "413" as "four one three" rather than "four hundred thirteen". "Pos[413]" means fourth floor, first aisle, third row.

- Resolve a frustrated transposition – When the frustrated transposition is an attempt to transpose by comparing slabs[Row] rotated 90 degrees clockwise, for example, resolving the frustration is accomplished by finding that a list of cubes in slabs[Floor] of the solution rotated from is the same as a list of cubes in slabs[Aisle] of the solution being rotated to. See "Frustrated transposition".

- Rotate slabs – Turn the solution around an imaginary line that runs through its center. The imaginary line is perpendicular to the slabs of cubes being rotated. For rotating cubes in slabs[Floor] the imaginary line is vertical. For rotating cubes in slabs[Aisle] the imaginary line is horizontal from left to right. For rotating cubes in slabs[Row] the imaginary line is horizontal from front to back. In rotating a solution, all the cubes are moved to new positions. However, when a gizmo is rotated on slabs[Floor] the cubes in slab[Floor 1] remain in slab[Floor 1], cubes in slab[Floor 2] remain in slab[Floor 2], etc. Rotating cubes in slabs is an action used in transposing a solution from one octant of origin to another.

The Glossary

- Rotational paths or paths of rotation – There are nine paths of rotation from a solution, three paths per coordinate. For the Floor coordinate the paths are "cubes in slabs[Floor] rotated 90 degrees clockwise", "cubes in slabs[Floor] rotated ninety degrees counterclockwise", and "cubes in slabs[Floor] rotated 180 degrees".

- Rotationally equivalent digital solutions – When transposing by rotating cubes in slabs[Floor], for example, rotational equivalence is demonstrated between two solutions when the lists of cubes in slabs[Floor] in the two solutions are the same. An additional test is required to resolve a frustrated transposition.

- Seeds – Cube[1] and cube[2], or the positions of cube[1] and cube[2] in a solution or in a path of solution..

- Sequence of Generation – Harry can generate two unique digital solutions from each pair of seeds in Alpha Class and six unique digital solutions from each pair of seeds in Beta Class. One of Harry's inputs is the name of the sequence-of-generation that is <u>desired</u> as output. The names are the ordinals "First", "Second", "Third", . . . "Sixth". Starting with a pair of seeds, Harry generates solutions in sequence ending his work with the generation of the <u>desired</u> sequence. A solution or a path of solution is identified by the positions of its seeds and its sequence of generation.

- Slab and slab[Row 1] – A slab is like a slice of cake from a square cake. It is a section of the 4x4x4 array of spaces. It is a 1x4x4 array with all its sixteen positions having the same value in one of its coordinates. For example, the front of the 4x4x4 array is a slab. It is slab[Row 1]. It consists of the sixteen cubic spaces with the coordinate "Row" having the value 1, or it is the sixteen cubes in those spaces. See "External Slab".

The Glossary

- Slabs[Floor], Slabs[Aisle], Slabs[Row] – There are four slabs of Floor, one slab for each value of the Floor coordinate. "Slabs[Floor]" is a list of all sixty-four cube numbers, grouped in the list such that the sixteen cubes in slab[Floor 1] are grouped together, the sixteen cubes in slab[Floor 2]are grouped together, etc. The list is obtained by using Excel's "sort" command to sort one of Harry's digital solutions with the primary sort key being "coordinate[Floor] *smallest to largest*" and the secondary sort key being "cube number *smallest to largest*". "Slabs[Floor] *inverted*" is obtained in the same way with "coordinate[Floor] *largest to smallest*". See "Inverted Slabs."

- Straight cube – A cube in the snake in which the elastic string exits the cube through the face of the cube that is opposite from and parallel to the face of its entry. The elastic string goes straight through the cube. See "Corner Cube".

- Translate a Solution – Reverse the cube numbers in Harry's digital solutions to match the ordering of the cubes as specified in the digital solutions provided by Creative Crafthouse.

- Transpose by rotation – Transpose a solution from one octant of origin to another. Transpose by rotation is a process used in identifying the twenty-four paths of solution in a family of solutions. "Transposing" is another name for the process "Determining rotational equivalence".

- Ultimate corner – A position in the 4x4x4 array. There are eight ultimate corners as follows: 111, 114, 141, 144, 411, 414, 441, 444.

- Visual anchor – An aid to physically, rather than digitally, solving the King Snake puzzle. The visual anchor is the cube, or the segment of cubes, with position set during the first steps in solving the puzzle. Then, understanding how to orient and place each cube[n] comes from comparing Harry's prescribed position for cube[n] to the set position of the visual anchor.

www.ingramcontent.com/pod-product-compliance
Lightning Source LLC
LaVergne TN
LVHW061953050326
832904LV00010B/300